DENEQUE WHITE & LINDA
GRINVALSKY

Hood Starseed

The Life of Deneque White: Part 1

First edition

ISBN: 979-8-9909330-0-2

Editing by Linda Grinvalsky

This book was professionally typeset on Reedsy.
Find out more at reedsy.com

I would like to thank Linda for going through this journey with me and Elias, Rosalie, and Sameer for giving me the strength to share my story.
−Love Memaw

Contents

Foreword

1974, the year it all started. The beginning, the big bang, the happening, simply the birth. A beautiful baby. Isn't that what they always say, beautiful baby boy, beautiful baby girl? But that's not how life always turns out.

This, of course, is not my opinion on the matter. Most of what you will read I do not agree with, but I may have a few biases. This will mainly work on fact as much as the memory will allow.

To be clear, these are not my memories. These are the memories of the woman who raised me. My mother. I would like you to understand that this is not a simple task for me and I don't expect it to be a simple task for you. I appreciate you taking the time to read this. Understand that it does have a happy ending, even when it doesn't seem like it could happen.

This is a love story. More importantly, this is a self-love story, which took a lifetime to achieve with multiple different types of heartbreaks and abuse to overcome. I hope this helps you in some way in your life, even if that's just being grateful that this didn't happen to you. This is one of the hardest things I've had to do because this is very personal to me, but for the sake of the readers, I am determined to complete this project.

It is commonly thought that trauma is what people remember in the most detail. Whether accurate or not, trauma has a certain hold on people. Though how long that span of trauma has before it fades, I do not know. Can it be a traumatic hour or day? Can it last for weeks or months? We are going to test this theory.

I will do my best to be as honest and subjective as possible. To protect the person's identity and respect their privacy, we will change some names. At this point, I have not heard everything. But I know it will be interesting, to say the least, and I will try not to omit any details for your benefit. I would feel misleading if I started this on a jolly note. Rather, I would like to start this with more of a warning. Don't get me wrong, this is not a simple tactic of reverse psychology. I just want to be honest.

With that said, if you are faint of heart or have issues with verbal or physical abuse, domestic, child and animal, suicide, rape, or drugs, I would kindly suggest reading something a bit lighter. This book is not kid-friendly, it is X-rated for violence. Don't get me wrong, this story does end on a more positive note, but like most illnesses, it gets worse before it gets better. Please take my words seriously and if that's all and you still want to continue, I will oblige.

1

Chapter 1

Dear Daughter,

I'm know I'm asking you to do this cuz you're the only one I trust
to write my story, but I'm sorry to put you through this. You're
strong and so intelligent, but there are things that happened
that are probably best kept in the darkest parts of my memory.
Sharing your story is supposed to be therapeutic and I need
something.

How I feel now is the best I have ever felt in my life. I'm closer
to my spirituality and closer to feeling like the true me than I
even thought possible. It's time to clear my name and set the
right things that have been wrong and unspoken. At anytime
during this process, if you want to stop, then I won't blame you
or think any less of you. This is the hardest thing I have ever
done and I know that after you hear everything, you might not
think it to be true, but it is the hardest thing for me to share these
things with you. I don't want to put this pain and confusion on
anyone, especially you.

This story is meant to help whomever it can and to help me get over some of the fear I've held inside.

2

Chapter 2

Dear Daughter,

I was born in mid-February 1974. It was one of the coldest
winter nights of the year. The snow piled up knee high, burying
cars completely. Getting around the city was nearly impossible.
I still hate the cold. Most people tend to prefer the weather in
which they were born. On the other hand, the cold tries to kill
me. Unfortunately, it seems that things I should love or enjoy
don't tend to feel the same, but you'll know more about that
later. As you well know, I wear three layers of clothes in the
spring. I can't take the heat either. I hate the heat.

I melt in the summer.

I do like the fall though. It's my favorite season.

My mother was 19 when she became pregnant and gave birth
to me at the age of 20. This is not very uncommon in the family
or the 70s, but her getting pregnant after her first time was a
shock to her more than anyone else. Despite using protection,
it didn't work. Her father was not happy as you could imagine
and did not speak to her for most of her pregnancy. Because he

had his room, that he didn't share with his wife, and went out often made this very easy.

The night I was born was a much-awaited occasion in the projects. The entire neighborhood was outside that day, well, not outside. They were hanging outside the project windows waving and cheering her on like it was some kind of big event.

They yelled, "Congratulations, congratulations" and she was waving like the Queen of the projects while getting in an ambulance. It must have been too funny. She, of course, must have already been in an incredible amount of pain, but my mother loved attention and admiration from any and everyone. She probably didn't even feel it over the rush of adrenaline she felt at seeing a crowd just for her.

After cautiously maneuvering through the terrible conditions of the road with a screaming pregnant woman in the back, the ambulance finally made it to the Queens General Hospital, and she said she was in the most pain in her entire life. In one hour, she had a baby girl named Deneque Sia McClain.

My dad named me. He was a five percenter; an Asiatic black man. Which is why he gave me that name.

His nickname was Dahu. He looked it up in some book and he thought it was a cool name. I don't know if it's a man's name. I'm not sure, but it means king or lord or something.

Sia is my middle name, which is after Mia Farrow, the actress whom he had a crush on. But he didn't want to name me Mia, of course, because he didn't want my mother to feel any type of way. So he thought he would switch the M with an S and hope she wouldn't notice. She didn't.

I was born with twelve fingers, six on each hand, and I was 7 lb even.

I came out so dark that my grandmother said she thought I

was one of my mother's friends' baby, which is hilarious. I was darker than both of my parents. Of course, everyone dismissed the claim, since she never slept with anyone except my father.

My dad was in jail, so my mother gave birth to me alone. I don't think they had men in the delivery room, but even if they did, he wouldn't have been there with her, anyway. He might have been in the hospital, but he would not have wanted to see that side of her, screaming and bleeding. They would put young girls in a ward, so they brought her to me.

My whole family came to see me, but when my aunt, my mother's older sister, and her husband saw me, she noticed I had six fingers on both of my hands. She cried. I guess she thought I was some kind of freak and my mother told the doctor to remove the fingers. So, they took a string and wrapped it around the base of them and they fell off.

I thought for so long that I was a freak for being born like that. It took years to realize I wasn't. At a family reunion, I met one of my cousins, who was born with extra fingers and toes. He kept all of his extra digits, while my hands only have small bumps on the sides where they used to be.

I remember you used to play with them and take some strange form of comfort from them. Probably just a way of also knowing that it was me.

I found out that it actually runs in the family. It would have been nice if someone told me sooner, but that's neither here nor there. I don't remember it but I heard that I cried to no end, so I guess it did hurt. That was my introduction to the world and pain.

My father was in prison with my uncle, my mother's brother, when I was born. I don't know if it was for robbery. I'm not sure, the story has changed so many times over the years.

I know it was my uncle, my dad, my mom's cousin, and a friend of my uncle. I suppose someone else initially intended to be there, but they backed out, so my father took their place and it led to a shootout. When they were leaving the store, the cops arrived before they could get away, so the driver left them behind.

My cousin left and my uncle got shot in the head. He was about 20 years old. My dad was 23. My dad ran back to my uncle because he called to him saying, "Please don't leave me, please don't leave me".

Feeling sad and scared that his friend was going to die, he ran back and held his hand, putting pressure on his wound and told him, "Stay with me. It's going to be alright". They both ended up going to prison, and my uncle survived. They stayed lifelong friends.

I don't know how I feel exactly about my dad going to jail. It was always something that I was used to. Never really something I put too much thought into—more of a fact of life. Sometimes I wish that maybe he would have been there for my mom. It would have been better. Maybe the idea of having a two-parent household sounds better. There is nothing wrong with being raised by a single mother. Plus, she wasn't even the only person who was in my life. There were so many people around me as a child that it didn't seem like I was missing out. I don't know what I would have missed because he wasn't there when he got out, anyway.

Only when I was older, I came to find out about his traumas and mental health, but being in a black family, those things aren't as taken care of as they are now. If he was considered functional on a basic level, they left him to his own devices.

I wasn't much raised by my mother either, so I don't know

how everything would have turned out if they were both present.

But, you know, I'm glad it happened the way it did because he wouldn't have been there to save my uncle. My grandma glorified him when I was younger because he saved her son. People have talked about him as a hero for as long as I can remember. I know now that what they were doing was wrong, but as a child, I only saw the loyalty and bravery that came with his actions and not the fact that they were stealing.

Maybe I wouldn't have had so many daddy issues that I noticed later on in life. I was looking for a father figure in all the wrong places.

He got out of jail when I was three, but he was always in and out of my life. I did have my uncle Buddy, who was like a father to me. I guess it's not the same as having a father that was there sometimes.

I probably have some abandonment issues and some other shit. I don't know I'll ever be able to deal with, but that's whatever.

Being the person that he was, then I probably would have come out worse than I did. He was young and only looking for a fast fuck. He didn't want a family. Because I was not his first child. I probably saw him more than my older sister did. It's not like we grew up together. The last time he saw her, she was six months old.

I'm glad he stayed with my Uncle James because then he wouldn't have had my cousin Lil James, whom I love dearly. Uncle James, when he wasn't high or before he got really deep into drugs, paid me a lot of attention, which I'm still grateful for. I know the injuries he had led to a lot of his drug use and he kind of got lost in it all.

My mother never put my dad on the birth certificate, so it just had her and me. I think she preferred it that way. She was never a very emotional person and I know I was not planned. She knew the type of person he was and wouldn't have intentionally tried to have a child with him. To be bound to him for the rest of her life is probably a nightmare she still has. I think it's funny. To have parents who have a love-hate relationship from the time they met. It is toxic, don't get me wrong, I know that, but again, it is something I'm used to.

3

Chapter 3

Dear Daughter,

After I came home from the hospital, everyone was excited to look at the new baby, but no one more than my grandfather. My grandfather adored me. He bought me a New York Mets doll. He loved the Mets. That was his favorite baseball team. He didn't speak to my mother the whole time she was pregnant. He was very upset with her, but when she brought me home, he couldn't wait to see me. My grandfather didn't even know she was pregnant until she was six months in. He only found out when she was reaching up to grab something in a high cabinet and saw her stomach.

He asked my grandmother "Is that girl pregnant?".

"Yes". That's all she said.

When my mother was worried about is all she said was "There's nothing he can do about it now".

I guess at the time he stopped running in the streets. I'm not sure if it was because he was getting older, or if it was because he was becoming a grandfather. Either way, that is when he started going to church, and all the love that he should have put into his wife and children he put into me. I always heard that he was not a good husband and father, but that was hard for me to see when he gave so much of his attention and cared for me. When I used to cry, he would yell at my mother and grandmother, he said, "Why won't you go pick that baby up? That baby back there cryin'".

They said, "No, we don't want to pick her up cuz then she'll be spoiled".

He thought they were crazy. Sometimes he'd even break down and pick me up himself and hand me to my mother. I don't know if it just broke his heart that I was crying or if it was the fact that they were ignoring me.

When I started to walk around at one or two years old, he doted on me. He said he loved me to death and would take me to the store. I sat on his lap and watched baseball games and I do remember as a toddler how he kept saying, "When you get a little bigger, Imma taking you to a Mets game".

He never took his kids, never took his wife, but he said it to me. I didn't understand the game, of course. I think I just enjoyed sitting on his lap. It felt like home. He started bringing me chocolates from the candy store every day. To this day, I love chocolate and all kinds of chocolate. Chocolate bars, mainly because he knew I probably would choke on anything else.

He used to roast peanuts in the oven all the time. He loved roasted peanuts, and my cousin and I would always try to sneak and take some. We were little toddlers grabbing it right out of the oven. It smelled so good from inside the oven. We would stand waiting for it to be done, but we never quite waited long enough. It would scorch our hands every time, but I guess because we were small, we didn't care. He would yell till the ceiling shook, but he never put his hands on us.

I looked up at him so much that I started to imitate him. I would put on kids' shades and take my grandmother's purse, put on a long housecoat, and pretend I was him coming home from work. He would always wear a long trench coat that was at least 3XL. He was not a fat man; instead he was very skinny and tall.

Most of the men in my family tend to be at least 6 feet tall. I believe he was about 6'4. As a child, you have to imagine he looked like a giant. He also wore a fedora. Sometimes he would have a briefcase. I don't know why since he was a mechanic, but he'd work as a janitor at Queens College sometimes.

I believe he had so much love inside him that near the end of his life; it was like a will. He figured if he can't take it with him, might as well give it to someone. Thank God I was the lucky recipient of all that never-ending love.

I do feel bad that he didn't give it to my grandmother or any of his children, but I did get to experience it for at least five years. After he passed, it wasn't the same. I miss him as a father figure. My dad never came around.

4

Chapter 4

Dear Daughter,

The first time he came to take me for a day I was three, from what my mother told me. I don't remember, but I guess he came by to pick me up and I started crying because I didn't want to go with him. I didn't know who he was, and that started an argument between my mother and my dad.

She said, "She doesn't know you".

He assumed that my mother turned me against him, but that wasn't it. I didn't know it, but he got locked up while my mother was pregnant. I did visit him all the time, but I thought it was like a playground. Like you know a park. I realized later on that it was family day at the prison.

I look at pictures now and it all makes sense, but as a child, I just knew that I was with my dad. I didn't realize how he always wore the same clothes or why we only visited him at the same place and that he never came to see me.

Anyway, I don't know if I was just upset because I was going with my dad or if it was because my mother wasn't coming with us. I was always up under my mother. If I was going outside, I was always with my mother or my grandmother. I don't think I was scared of him, per se. I was upset that my mother wasn't coming too. Like, I'm not going to go if my mother's not coming. She has to come or I'm not going, and I screamed and had a tantrum as toddlers do.

I didn't see him again till a few years later, but my mother always took me to my grandmother, his mother, to try to spend the night. I slept in the bed with my grandmother and my aunt. During the day I was fine, but at bedtime, I'd start screaming to no end. It wasn't that I didn't like spending time over there, I just wanted my mother. I thought my grandmother was funny, and I loved to be around her. She also loved to curse and liked to take me to the movies.

It became normal for me not to see my dad for long periods of time. He was never very reliable for sticking around, but he was always very good at disappearing. If he did not want to be found, then he just wasn't. You have to wait for him to appear like a groundhog on Groundhog Day. This just sometimes took years to where I wouldn't wait for him and when he did show up, you just don't get your hopes too high. As a child, this was hard, but again, he wasn't there.

By the time I was old enough to realize that he should have been there, I already had other people in my life who filled his role. It isn't the same, of course, but I think it was for the best. It might have been better for me if he wasn't there at all. You can't miss something you never had or someone who was never there.

5

Chapter 5

Dear Daughter,

When I came home from the hospital, my mother was living with her parents and her two brothers. My cousin, who wound up living with us later, would come over and spend nights with us, so I did have someone to play with. I was a year older than her; we were born the same month and a week apart, which I thought was cool because our parents are twins.

My aunt got married in '72 to Buddy. Whom I loved dearly. My grandmother loved to talk about how when my aunt was a young girl he was in the Korean war. They were only ten years apart. But you know how black people love to be colorful. He didn't like talking about his time in the war much, but I know that he was stationed in Korea and he left me everything, including his souvenirs, when he passed. He also used to talk about how he loved fly-fishing.

Then next was my uncle James, who was a year older than my mother and my uncle. I can't imagine what my grandmother went through with my aunt running the streets as a pre-teen

14

and with three babies at home. She was a maid, you know, for rich people, but she always kept a clean house. Maybe that's part of her training. I witnessed her juggling multiple jobs and making sure that all of us were taken care of.

She had a seventh-grade education, but an education really couldn't do much, anyway. As a girl, she loved school but had to stop attending in order to help provide for her family. Many children at this time had to do this cause it was the great depression.

She was one out of twelve children, so dealing with many children at one time wasn't something new in her life. She watched her parents do it. It is very uncommon for people in the family to have no children. Most have at least four children.

Most people in the family live till at least 90, so growing up with your great grandparents is normal for us. It's weird, but in our blood line we always outlive our spouses. If you marry into the family, you're died.

Men or women, it doesn't matter we always live longer than those who we marry.

The women in our family usually live longer than the men. Even though the men in the family can live through amazing feats. They can get shot, stabbed, or beaten and they always end up dying from a heart attack or cancer years later. They still outlast their spouses.

My grandmother was always a very strong-willed person and achieved what she put her mind to.

Black women did not have many rights anyway and even if she was college educated, finding a career would have been near impossible. My grandfather had a sixth-grade education, even with little to no education. They owned a candy store and a restaurant in the late 50s and all through the 60s which was a miracle. I always respected her for that, and it's probably where I get my grind and hustle from. She encouraged me to never give up on anything that I wanted, no matter the odds.

Anyway, at home it was cool. I watched a lot of TV; you know, mainly kid stuff like Sesame Street. I was very excited to get to watch cartoons because it wasn't like now where you can watch cartoons all day. We had to wait for cartoons once a week, for a Saturday morning cartoon, like Space Coaster on Channel 13, which was still a big deal. Plus, they cut off the cartoons at 10 am. We got five hours of cartoons a week and we had to wake up at 5 am to catch it.

I was young, so I usually watched what the adults watched, which was mainly soap operas. I remember being about two or three years old, not knowing what I was looking at, but the adults tended to leave the TVs on.

They played a lot of music when I was about three and four. I would watch them sing and dance. My uncle Lenny, my mother's twin, would mainly sing the Temptations. I guess I held onto those memories because even my kids know all the greatest hits of the Temptations. I remember have you guys sing and dance in the living room. You even performed "My Girl" at a talent show and won. I'm still so proud of all of you.

My uncle James was more into Eddie Kendrick and Smokey Robinson. He had a very light voice, like Eddie Kendrick. Now my mother likes a good deal of music. She made me a disco person. She was an amazing singer and mainly focused on opera. If it wasn't for her stage fright, she could have gone a long way.

6

Chapter 6

Dear Daughter,

I remember my earliest clear memory when I was four, and she wanted me to go to preschool. My mother took me there and the first day the parent stayed all day. I loved to be around other kids and have all those toys to play with.

Being an only child, I became accustomed to playing by myself. I did play with my cousin when she came over, but at first she didn't live with us. I didn't know how to play with other kids. It took some time. I was nervous, but also very excited.

It felt like being at the park because whenever I looked, my mother was there watching me and I felt safe. It was cool. I went to the pre-school at the end of the projects. That's where all the kids went. It's like a rite of passage or something.

The second day, I didn't know she was only going to stay half a day. She never told me she was going to leave. She placed me on my cot and I was peeping while watching her. It wasn't that I didn't trust her. I just liked knowing that she was there and sleeping in a room with other children is something to get used to.

She was standing with the teacher near the door. I wasn't sleepy, no kids slept at nap time. I laid there and then I saw my mother walk out the door.

I was like, where is she going? Oh my God, she's not leaving me here. I jumped up and ran for my mother saying "Mommy Mommy". The teachers grabbed me.

I started kicking and screaming, trying to get to my mother. I broke free by kicking the teacher in the leg. She let me go and I tried to chase her down the block. I caught up with her but she told me "Oh no, you have to go back".

I cried, "Don't keep me there, don't leave yet". She spoke to the teacher and grabbed my stuff and said they'll bring me back the next day. Well, she took me home and told my grandmother what happened.

My grandmother said, "She's not ready yet".

The next day, I knew I'd have to go back to school. When I went back, I walked in there, so scared. There were so many kids and so many toys. I did like the toys. It all felt different knowing that she was going to leave me there, though. It didn't feel so safe. I didn't feel any kindness from the pre-school teachers that day. I only stayed for a about an hour so my mother could talk to the teacher and see what was going to be done about how I was acting. The teacher said that I was not ready and should wait for another year. My mother was pissed. She took me home, and I was so happy. I thought I didn't have to go to school anymore after that. I did start school the next year, but I was happier to go then.

My kindergarten teacher was Mrs. Carter. She was so sweet to me. She just felt motherly. I wasn't as scared as the year before. She made me feel safe and cared for to the point when I was dropped off that first day I saw and she took my hand and I just went with her. I didn't school for my mother or cry. I was happy to go with her. I played with a lot of toys and I made friends. I loved school them, but that was the best school year I ever had.

By the time I was five years old, the kids in the neighborhood were cool and I had a lot of friends. Usually, kids you know are kids from the block. How to meet them is usually through the adults. Your parents and grandparents know their parents and grandparents. My grandmother was the first person to move into those projects, so everyone moved in around her.

The adults on the block called me Little Linda because a lot of them didn't know how to pronounce my name or couldn't be bothered to learn. Which is rude, ain't it?

Some of them will just call me Pockets. Like ... "Come here Pockets". They would say Pockets ...and at the time, I didn't think anything of it. When I got older, I found out my mother gave me that nickname because she complained that it was hard to get me pants. After all, I wasn't shaped like her. My mother was 5'3 paper bag color. If anybody knows what that means, medium chest, a small waist, and a big butt, you can put a glass on and she wouldn't even know that it's there.

I guess you can say like the women nowadays who pay to get the BBL, as they call it. My mother was natural, with great legs and pretty feet.

As for me, I am a chestnut brown, more like Angela Bassett's complexion. As a child, of course, I didn't have any chest, and I didn't have the black girl booty, as you call it. So, she always complained that it was hard to find me pants.

She would tell people. Even as a child, you can see I was never gonna be shaped like her. I was very thin and my pants used to fall a lot. I always had to hear her talking to the women on the

19

bench about me. She was in her twenties and cared more about what people thought and said about the projects. She thought that at five years old people would ask why I didn't have a butt, so she decided to offer up an explanation and started the nickname for me. I found that out when I was in my thirties. That still hurts me. She started to make fun of me before anyone else could. It was not for my benefit, though it was for her own.

I felt okay about the nickname then, but I was hurt when I found out why I got that name... which came years later. A lot of kids had nicknames back then. We had a kid with a wooden leg we called Woody and brothers, who each had one eye. They both lost their eyes on the fourth of July putting rockets in a glass bottle. Instead of shooting up, the rocket tipped the bottle and fell over and hit one brother in the eye and the next year the other brother looked over the bottle to see why the rocket didn't ignite. It was just wet, so it took longer and when he leaned over to see what was wrong, it hit him straight in the eye.

They were called Cyclops One and Cyclops Two. The names stuck with them till adulthood for all except me. The nicknames weren't very creative, but it made sense.

People can be cruel. I didn't see a problem with their names either when I was that age. I never thought they didn't like it. I fought to change my nickname, which in the projects is almost impossible.

Woody was born with one leg. I think as he got older; he had the prosthetic leg people have today. But to us, he would always be Woody.

Anyway, my pants would always slide down. My mom would say … "she doesn't have a butt so I call her Pockets because that's all she is back there … pockets". That made the women on the bench laugh and that name stuck until I was about 12 years

20

old.

Around the time people started calling me Pockets, my grandfather passed away.

When my grandfather died, I remember not going to the funeral. I guess they didn't let me go because I was too little, but afterward, the repast was at my grandmother's house. So many people came. Wall to Wall family and friends and people from the neighborhood. I couldn't believe some of the people who came. They barely spoke to my grandmother in the street, but hung out with my grandfather. I just wanted these people to leave cuz they were laughing and joking and I guess it seemed disrespectful that he was gone and everyone seemed so happy.

They were enjoying catching up with each other because a lot of them hadn't seen each other in years. As a kid, I saw these crowds of people like tourists in Times Square taking in the sights and having a great time, While I was in deep pain.

I wished my grandfather would just walk through the door smiling at me, put me on his knee, give me a piece of chocolate from the candy store, and tell me about his day. I just wanted the people to leave. Maybe I even wanted them to cry because that would at least prove that they were really sad. It would make more sense. Misery likes company and on that day I was miserable, but worst of all, I felt alone.

How could you laugh at a time like this? I just wanted to go on into my room and close the door. I did go hide in my room near the end, after all the phony introductions to people I didn't give a damn about were over. I went to my room and tried to lie on my bed, but you know how it was back in the day. People would put their coats in the back bedroom and just tell people to lay them on the bed. Well, that was my bed smelling of everyone's coats. From cheap perfume to old man cologne to cigars and cigarettes, alcohol and mothballs.

So many coats on my bed I just wound up laying on top of them. There were so many of them I didn't feel like moving them. Plus, someone would have had a fit if their coat was found on the floor. People would be less offended to find a child sleeping on their stuff than it touching the floor. Then again, it is bad luck to have certain things lying on the floor like a wallet or purse, anyway.

I fell asleep on top of the coats, weird smells and all. My grandmother woke me up at the end of the repast by hitting me on the legs, "get off these people's coats so they could go home".

I got up, but I was thinking, why were their coats on my bed in the first place? But I knew better that to talk back to her. When everyone grabbed their things and left the house, it all...felt different.

After he passed, I started going over to his mother's house. She was still alive then. She passed in '81. My great-grandmother was a very light-skinned woman. I thought she was a white lady. Her house was always dark, and she used to sit in a chair all the time. People used to come over and stand around her like she was a shine to stare at and praise. I rarely saw her get up from that chair. It was a big recliner.

You walk through the front door and as soon as you enter it, there's the foyer, then right in front of you are these big stairs that lead to the upstairs bedrooms and bathroom. It's funny how big the stairs seem to me then. In my memory, it seemed that the stairs went on forever. And the higher they got, the darker it got. I was so scared to look up when I went there. It was dark even when it was daytime.

At five, it looked like a haunted house.

After my grandfather died, I started to go over there a lot

because my great-grandmother wanted to see me. I was the oldest grandchild of his ...at the time. I'll tell you about that later.

If I turned to the right, there was a living room or the parlor that they called it. She sat in the chair off the center of the room and she would say, "Come here, Arthur's grand baby". Everybody would part like the Red Sea and have me walk through a gauntlet of adults.

I would have to walk up to her and hug her. She would squeeze me like she never squeezed before. Like she was trying to squeeze the life out of me. She had like an old black wig that was a little scratchy, you know, with curls that were smashed together like she forgot to shake it out to loosen up the curls after taking it out of the box. It was scratchy because it was old. I loved the hugs now that I think about it. They were great, but you know sometimes family will squeeze kids a little too long, but it was fine because I knew she did love me.

My grandfather had siblings. There was his brother David Jr. who died before I was born. I don't know too much about him. Then my Uncle Kenny, my grandfather's other brother. He was cool and he would come to my grandmother's house a lot. He was always in the military. He was in every war since WWII. He was a sergeant and then he was in the Reserves, never got married, and had no kids. He never got hurt in war, not once, but later on in the late 80s he died of cancer. It's funny how he survived every war and finally came out of the service and died of a sickness.

Then there was my Aunt Alice and my Aunt Dale. Aunt Alice was nice and her kids used to come to my grandmother's house often to hang with their cousins, mainly her sons, to hang out with my uncle James and the twins.

Anyway, my aunt Dale didn't have any children but always had a beer or would smell like beer even when she didn't have a beer in her hand. She cussed like a sailor and she was funny as hell. She was my favorite on that side. I don't know why, maybe because she cursed, but she was funny to me. It's like she didn't hold her tongue, so every time she yelled at somebody or talked I used to be amazement at the profanity that would come out of her mouth. She said words and put phrases together that I didn't know were possible.

For example, she would call someone a shoe horned face mother fucker or a turkey fucker, then tell the next person to eat a pig nut sandwich. When she was happy she would say well fuck a duck, I just hit the number. A lot of animal references maybe because they came from the south. Either way, can you see how colorful her vocabulary was and how, to this day, I don't like farms or zoos?

Another aunt was Essie Mae, his youngest sister. She was truly religious, like her mom; she was a well-known evangelist. She passed away a few years ago. I know you remember her. Even in her coffin she was grinning cause she knew where she was going.

She was very sweet. It was wonderful that all my kids were old enough to meet and talk to her. I loved her as well and I remember her running the candy store.

7

Chapter 7

Dear Daughter,

My grandmother and my grandfather had the candy store. As I was told, she lost the restaurant. My grandfather's siblings (not Aunt Dale, who passed by this time, and not Essie Mae, but she owned the candy store with my grandparents) came over with paperwork and found out they kind of tricked him into signing it away. They told him they would make sure his family would have equal shares of it so his wife and kids would be taken care of.

Come to find out, he winds up signing it all away. Aunt Alice and Uncle Kenny took the store, but when Uncle Kenny died, it all went to Aunt Alice and her children.

The restaurant my grandmother tried to keep for years without any help from her husband or his family. Much as she could hold on to it, it didn't help that my grandfather used to go to the restaurant any time of the day (which I always heard was busy), take money from the register, and leave. He would spend the money on women and alcohol and whatever was in the street.

My grandmother would have to leave the restaurant if she didn't have enough change in the register to give customers and go across the street or next door to different businesses just to make the change.

The restaurant was so busy that my mother had to work there a couple of summers to help out and get extra money for school clothes or you know, money for her pocket. My grandmother's restaurant was open from late afternoon to evening during the weekdays, and all day on weekends. She still worked as a maid during the day.

My mother's siblings didn't work there. I'm not sure too much about what they did except that my Uncle James would be in the street hustling drugs or whatever or doing little things in the street to make his money. I know my aunt worked in an office building downtown for a few years until she got hurt in an elevator accident and sued and never had to work again. My mother's twin chased girls and tried to be the next Marvin Gaye.

My aunt Essie Mae, I do know in the mid-80s she still had the candy store. As far as what my grandmother did, she worked as a maid. She said she was a live-in maid after she lost the restaurant. She'd only work Monday through Saturday. Then, during the weekend, she would work and go to church every Sunday.

She had to hire a nanny to take care of her children while she was at work cuz her husband wasn't home. Bunny used to watch her younger siblings, but then she had a party once when her mother was working. She put her siblings in the back room and told them to stay there and be quiet. They wanted to join the party even though they were only about ten. They couldn't join the party so they told their mother when she got home and, of course bunny got in trouble and she hired a nanny.

Their father would be sleeping or out. The nanny she hired would cook and clean and watch the children while she worked. My grandfather didn't care. They basically hired a second wife. The nanny only came over on Saturday cuz during the week there was school. Some Sundays she went to work after church if the people she worked for needed her for a party or some other event.

She would insist that me and my cousin also attended church. It was a mandatory activity that I think every black child who had a family from the south had to endure. I liked going to church. Maybe it was the friends that I had or that I was so used to going that it became a natural spring of comfort for me. Back then, you would be in church every day of the week. After I was born, she was retired and I guess she didn't know what to do with her time, so we would just go to church. She was so used to going outside that she wanted to do something that she felt was productive, and that was what church was. Every day would be a distinct thing, like bible study or choir practice. I even had to go to bible camp in the summers.

Money was going to unnecessary things, and they barely had food. Money was tight. To this day, my mother still doesn't eat oatmeal because my grandmother used to get mush all the time, the nasty porridge you see in the Little Rascals movie or the book Oliver Twist. She also has a strange fear of her cupboards being empty. There is always food in her house now. If the fridge even seems like a shelf might be empty by the next day, there will be a trip to the supermarket.

We had a lot of TVs in the house and in the kitchen we had 2. It's not what you think. One was on top of the other. The big one on the bottom would be channels 7, 9, 11, 13, and 21 and the small one on top would get channels 2,4 and 5, but it needed a wire coat hanger and aluminum foil for a clear picture.

The back bedroom which my grandmother, me, and my cousin shared had a 32 inch TV on top of the dresser facing both beds. My bed was on the left when you entered and my grandmother's bed was on the right. My cousin slept with my grandmother. I wondered why she never slept in the same room as my grandfather and when I asked she said, "He's a nasty man". I didn't really understand, but of course I know now. Again, he was someone I looked up to at the time and it was hard to see other than the caring, loving man I thought I knew so well.

That TV, well, all the TVs were black and white except the little one on top of the big one in the kitchen. The back bedroom TV did get all the channels, it's just it had no knobs. You had to turn the channel with pliers, which gave a loud popping sound every time you changed the channel, which made it difficult when you're trying to watch something that you were told not to watch. Shows that had adult content like the Benny Hill show which played on Channel 9. My grandmother kept the TV station on channels 5, 7, or 11 at all times for news, and on Saturday or Sunday movies, the news, wrestling, or kung fu movies. Channel 11 was mainly my mom. She liked Westerns and Tarzan pictures.

When we're in trouble and on time out, my grandmother would take the pliers. It was the most messed up thing that could happen. Then I would have to sit there and watch whatever was on the TV. My cousin would leave and go to her father's room, but I couldn't go in there. I would be pissed. It was the equivalent of taking the wires out of a TV now. We couldn't do shit. Where would I get pliers? I was a kid and she would hide them in her house coat front pocket? I would try to get them from her pocket when she was sleeping in the chair in the dining room, but I would have them halfway out and I would look up at her and she would be staring at me.

I was like, "Oh my God" and slowly push them back in. Then I would walk back to the room.

She would just as "mmmhhhmm" and go back to sleep. It was terrifying and she wouldn't say anything else. She really didn't have to.

I had a lot of toys and a lot of dolls. I had 10 of them. Being a part of a poor family in the 70s, that was considered a lot.

I had a little rocking chair; I had a cabin bed at the time and I had a toy chest that looked like a train that had a green roof on it like a rooftop, like you see on a gingerbread house with little circles on it. It was plastic and had animals on the side. My room was all Raggedy Anne and Andy. When I was old enough to realize my surroundings, I didn't know why the hell they chose this. I didn't like it. It was horrifying. Them just all over my room smiling at me.

Anyway, after kindergarten, which was an exceptional year, all I did was play. I made a couple of friends and learned how to play with others, which was nice cuz I was an only child, so it was great. You get lonely playing games by yourself all the time. That was the first summer that I went to Sabine, West Virginia. By this time, Buddy and Bunny moved down there because Buddy's mother and father were ill, so Buddy went back to being a coal miner. Which is what they did in that town, and Bunny helped his mother with housework.

It was great. That was the first time I was really in the country and they had a stream in the back of the house, or a creek, as they called it. It looked like something from a movie. You go straight down the driveway, go to the back of the house then you go down these little steps and open a gate and it's a creek with all these rocks which we had to be careful on cuz the rocks were slippery so I couldn't go too far.

The water that rolled down these rocks was so beautiful. The water was so clear that you could look down and see the fish swim by. There were also wildflowers that would grow around the rocks. It was beautiful and looked like something out of a movie.

The house was a two-story home. It was yellow and white and they had a pickup truck all silver and red with black stripes on the side. It looked like a race car that they turned into a truck. Mind you, this is 1979, so I thought they were rich.

There were not too many black people in the town. I think they were the only black ones. I remember a guy who lived on the left. His name was Bumblebee. He was a very short white guy, about 5 feet, who never wore a shirt or shoes. Mind you, there were only dirt roads. There were no paved streets like in the city. He used to just walk around barefoot.

Buddy, his older brother, Bumblebee, and another white guy in the town used to bet money on fights, but not just any fights. They had snake fights. Each of them would bring their prize-winning snake out into the middle of the road and see who attacked the other one first. They weren't venomous, at least the ones that were fighting with. Don't get me wrong, there were venomous snakes in the country.

I loved to watch the fights. Basically, how it worked was they placed the snakes in the middle of the road and whichever one bit the other first would win. They were not fighting to the death or anything like some other animal fights were back then. They wanted to have the fastest snakes, but they weren't trying to have them cause major damage to each other or anything. All you would see is snakes and dollar bills in the middle of the road pushing up dirt.

I had to sit in the back of the pickup truck with my little bunny rabbit, which I carried everywhere. She was a yellow bunny rabbit that was almost as big as me, and her name was Michelle.

I got there by plane. It was my first flight ever. I love to fly now, but that time I was nervous. My mother took me to the airport. It was me, my mother, and my grandmother. We went to LaGuardia Airport.

She took me to the airport. I didn't realize really what was going on. I was just thinking we were going out somewhere, as we usually do. But now we are at the airport. She hands me over to a lady with little wings on her jacket. The lady took my hand and led me away from my mother into a long hallway. I asked the lady, "Is my mother coming later?"

She asked, "No. there should be family waiting for you on the other side". I'm thinking on the other side of the tunnel. I was confused. I knew I was going to see my aunt, and I knew she didn't live in New York, but I was five and didn't know what a plane was or that I was getting on one. I just wanted my mother.

"Well, you're going to get on a gigantic bird that's going to go into the sky and when it lands your aunt and uncle will be there waiting for you".

"Okay". Isn't that horrifying, though? I mean, there was nothing I could do. I never went somewhere with a stranger before.

I found out later that my mother was terrified of planes and refused to come with me. The idea was "If the plane crashes, why do both of us have to die". I still don't fully understand her mind set about that and I don't think it would help me in any way to unpack that.

They put me on a window seat next to this nice lady who asked me if I was okay and if I wanted anything to eat. She asked me who I was going to see. I smiled, worked on my coloring book, and held tight to my bunny rabbit, Michelle. The plane takes off and we go up over New York. It looked so small from up there. I'm sitting right next to the window and all of a sudden we are in the clouds. In my mind, I was flying over heaven. It was the most beautiful thing I've ever seen. I've always gone to church with my grandmother and I have always been so close to God, but I have never been closer to God than that moment right there. I heard someone talking on the other side like I hope we don't crash or I hope the plane doesn't fall.

I didn't even think of that cuz I was like, if the plane does crash, it doesn't matter. I already know where I'm going. It's the most beautiful place I've ever seen. I figured I'd just go right back in the clouds, so I was already halfway there. To this day, I have to have the window seat.

The only bad part about the flight was my ears popping. My ears were killing me. They gave me a piece of gum, which helped a bit, but my jaw was killing me when I arrived in West Virginia from all the chewing.

When my uncle and aunt picked me up, they were standing there smiling, and they hugged me and we got in the car at Charleston West Virginia Airport and it took us 2 hours to get to their house. I threw up all the way there. I had carsickness, which also runs in the family. They had to stop multiple times at gas stations to clean out the car and let me go to the bathroom to clean up. That's how my first summer in West Virginia began and it would not be my last one.

8

Chapter 8

Dear Daughter,

I loved to go to see them. I had my New York friends and my west Virginia friends. It was like I had two lives and I think I liked the west Virginia one better. I am a city girl at heart, but there is something different about the country. The quiet and peace that comes with it is unmatched. There were dangers in the country like there are in all places, but the country seemed more manageable.

I also had Bunny and Buddy, which were more of my parents away from home. They took good care of me and showed that they loved me. Even as I got older, they treated me like a daughter. They could not have children of their own, so they adopted me in more ways than one. They even left everything for me in their will. I'm sad to say that I don't have much now of what they left me, but that's a story for later.

My mother was jealous of the relationship I had with her sister, but only a bit. My mother liked it when I was gone, if not only for the freedom it gave her to have summers without a child. In my family, this is not uncommon, though. The family is very big, but we do try to stay close and one way is by sending the children away to spend time with their cousins, even if that is in an unfamiliar state.

Some of my favorite memories are those summers in the country with Bunny and Buddy.

While I was in West Virginia, I learned a lot of things I never would have learned in New York. I learned how to fish and how to grow different vegetables. They had a pleasant garden at the back of the house. I loved it there. I even used to call my uncle and aunt, mom and dad. I knew they weren't my parents, but I always wished they were. I still consider my uncle my real father. My mother is in my life now and we talk very often, but that only started when I was an adult. I do wish I could have stayed there. My life would have been like the little house on the prairie. I used to idolize that show. Just how simple and easy everything was. Of course, they had their conflicts, but it was so much easier than being in New York.

It's strange cuz I knew that Buddy didn't like the country cuz he thought it was boring. I love being bored. I don't need all the drama and fighting or excitement. That's why he went to the war. He wanted to go to war cuz he was seventeen and wanted to get out of town when he had no money.

I don't think he was that disillusioned to think that war would be fun, but that it would be an experience. He did learn to hunt when he was in Korea. When he came back, he would hunt deer and other animals. He told me he learned how during the war and I was like, oh. I thought it was cool. I thought maybe they had deer in Korea. I learned later on that he was hunting people during the war. I was bugged out; I don't know. He didn't like talking about the war, but I know he was in the army.

Buddy's father used to tell me "I'm not your grandpa" every time I slipped and called him that, but then they always catered to me. He loved me. I used to follow him when he went down the creek. I do know that they had a basement that they entered into through the back door of the house where they had tools for skinning game and prepping food. They didn't allow me to go back there, but they hunted and fished most of the food we ate. I wasn't supposed to go down there because of all the knives and blood.

I would be so proud when they were very something, and I was not one of those kids who wanted them to throw the fish back in. I was excited knowing that we were going to eat it.

He would always chew tobacco. One day I stole a piece of tobacco just to be like him. Normally, you would chew the tobacco and spit out the juice. Well, I spit out the tobacco and swallowed the juice. I almost died. I was choking and when he found me he just said , "Good for you".

I got so sick I threw up and my nose was running and I had diarrhea for a few days. Buddy thought it was cute cause I was imitating his father. His father was mad that I chewed his tobacco, but he was worried about me. He was scared and wanted to take me to the hospital, but the other adults had confidence that I would be fine.

I knew he liked me and I didn't care that he always told me to go away. I knew he really liked me and I knew he was a good person. He was an old, very light-skinned man with glasses.

9

Chapter 9

Dear Daughter,

When I started going to Junior High, I started putting clothes in the toy chest. I did keep the dolls on the bed, though. My grandmother had a three-bedroom apartment. As soon as you walk into her apartment, there's a little coat closet on the right and on the left is the living room.

The living room was always blocked off with a chair that only moved when company came. All the furniture was covered with plastic. She had a little record player, but I believe it was my mom's. As you go to the living room, on the right-hand side, there is a kitchen that has a beautiful archway. As you enter the kitchen, which wasn't put together by glue or anything. No nails supported it, either. My grandfather stacked pieces of wood together like a game of Jenga. It was very sensitive, but it stayed there for years and he painted it. He painted over it with some brown paint, so maybe that would help it stay together, and it did.

My grandmother would put Nick-knacks all around it as well

as on the coffee table in the middle of the living room. On top of an oriental floor rug, she had a porcelain statue of Lassie that sat on the floor in the corner, which she loved. She always had plants in the window. Long plants, small plants, big plants, and spider plants. There were so many plants in the window that if your friends called you from outside, you could barely see them and if they tried to see you, it looked like a jungle. When I tried to look out the window, she would yell and say "Don't mess up my plants"

Then I would say, "Why are your plants in the window you can't even see? It looks like a jungle." Then she would pop me in my mouth to talk back.

She had a piano on the left of the living room covering the whole wall with family photos on top. It was my uncle James' piano that he got as a present from his godmother when he was a kid, my grandmother said. He played it sometimes, but it wasn't Mozart or anything. He played it less and less as he got older, but did know how to play a couple of tunes on it. He was good. If he kept going, he could have been great. By the time I came around the piano was just another Nick-knack that my grandmother dusted. I used to pretend to play by just banging on it. It was completely out of tune and it just sat there, but she always kept her living room clean. It was never dusty. He could also play the guitar and the saxophone. He was one of those kids who could hear a tune and play it.

My grandmother didn't want him to be a Nick-knack cuz she thought all musicians just do drug. He ended up on drugs anyway cuz he got shot.

There were pictures on the wall. Afro-centric pictures, you know, of the 70s versions of the black lady with an Afro. I found out Uncle James had made it when he went to prison. They were always there as far as I can remember and when I was five or six; they were on the wall. So, that showed me that he did it when I was a baby.

I remember one beautiful picture. There's a black woman with a chain around her neck and she was bending down on her knees. She was completely naked and facing her was a black man with an Afro with a chain around his neck. I'm not saying it's beautiful because of the chains. It was the Afro-centric artwork and the care to detail he put into it. It was glass and then it was like a glass stencil that was made with aluminum foil. Inside it was designed with bright colors and he made it by hand. The artwork in my grandma's house was all made by him. There was one with a black lady who looked like a panther. I thought they were amazing.

My mother, to this day, still has a couple of those pictures that he did in prison. He was talented. He wasn't one of those license plate-making inmates. He truly was an artist. His artistic skills were truly unmatched. If he lived during the Harlem Renaissance, he would have been named alongside Aaron Douglas and Jacob Law.

All my grandma's children were talented. My aunt Bunny, Voila Jr. (we called her Bunny because she was born near Easter). Before she got married, she was one of the members of the Cookies. Ray Charles's backup singers who eventually became the Raylettes. When Ray Charles came to New York, he wanted to sign the Cookies. My grandmother didn't want my aunt to go on tour, so she left the group because my grandmother didn't like secular music and heard about musicians doing devilish things on the road. So she didn't become a Raylette and gave up singing altogether.

My Uncle James wasn't just an artist, he also was a musician.

He could play the saxophone as well. In junior high, he was in the band.

I think after the shootout he had as a teen; he started taking drugs to ease the pain from his head. The doctor couldn't remove the bullet. If they tried to remove it, he could have died. He got headaches all the time, so he started abusing drugs to cope with the pain, which eventually became his downfall.

My uncle Lenny was talented too, also a singer. Lenny and his friend went on to perform at the Apollo on amateur night, which was known to make stars. They didn't win, but they didn't give up. He tried, but he was more into the ladies than anything. When his friend passed away when they were in their twenties, he gave up singing except in the living room or shower when he heard his favorite song play.

My mother had auditioned for Julliard to be an opera singer. Can you believe it? A black girl from the projects wanting to be an opera singer. My grandmother took her to the audition but my mother got stage fright when her name was called next to perform. When they left Julliard to head home, my grandmother told my mother, "I can't believe you didn't sing. I thought you were going to be somebody".

My mother was so sad and needed some words of kindness, but my grandmother wasn't the most sensitive person. My mother said she felt so low. That was a terrible thing to say to my mother. My grandmother was a devout Christian but wasn't very sensitive either.

I remember the story my mother told me when she went to work with my grandmother one time to clean the House of a white doctor that she worked for, for years. One day, my mother was at work to help her out. My grandmother was cooking and cleaning the rest of the house while my mother was cleaning the bathroom.

Out of nowhere, the son of the doctor (a teenager around my mom's age) asked my mother out on a date. It's not that she didn't like the guy or think he was unattractive. It's like my mother felt kind of resentful. Like how can you ask me out on a date when I'm on my knees scrubbing your bathroom floor?

I know a wave of anger came over her. She was so offended. The next thing you know, my grandmother lost her job with the doctor. I think my grandmother never forgave her. She didn't want my mother to go with him per se but blamed my mom anyway for losing a job she had for years instead of blaming the boy for being spiteful. My mother always did try to help my grandmother, but she always looked at her like a problem after that. I think that's why she favored her other kids over her.

Chapter 10

Dear Daughter,

My mother had had a dog since she was a kid. He was a German Shepherd mix. I'm not sure what he was mixed with, but she called him Shep. He was a big all-black dog with a chocolate brown coat underneath with white circles around his eyes. My cousin and I would try to ride him like a horse around the house, but we always fell because he didn't like it. My aunt had a little dog named Snowy. He was a white poodle. It was nice having animals in the house.

My uncles would be so mean to Shep. Shep would protect anyone in the house, but it didn't stop my uncles from abusing him while my mom was working. He didn't fight back or anything, no matter how much they beat him.

In the house were me, my little cousin who stayed permanently when she was around four years old, her dad; my Uncle Lenny, my grandmother, and Uncle James. At that time, my Aunt Bunny lived in Long Island City with her husband, Uncle Buddy, who became the next important man in my life after my grandfather. This is before they moved to the south.

My mother lived in a small one-bedroom apartment by herself. I would spend the night there some weekends if I begged long enough or if she wasn't having a party or a boyfriend over. Snowy lived with my aunt and uncle and died when I was 7 years old. After Snowy died, they seemed to get a dog every 3 to 5 years until I was an adult. They always had a dog, whether it was giving shelter to an abandoned dog or Buddy got a dog for hunting. Sometimes they even got a dog because they were dog-sitting and the owner never came to get them. I guess because they couldn't have children; they needed something to love and treated their dogs very well.

The hunting dogs came later when they moved to West Virginia.

Shep used to come up to me when I was a baby. My mother said he was very protective of me. When I used to cry, he used to lie next to me like most dogs do when a baby cries. When I started walking as a toddler, my mother would pop my hand and tell me "no" when I was doing something that I wasn't supposed to do as most do when they start exploring the world.

He growled at her and she said, "How dare you growl at me? I know you are not trying to bite the hand that feeds you?".

He always tried to protect me, no matter who it was. The adults in my house, other than my mother, would abuse him very badly. Like most dogs, he liked to sit in the doorway of the kitchen or bathroom and instead of stepping over him, they would kick him out of the way. It was not a nudge with their foot. They would kick him hard in the side or head. At any chance they got, they would stomp on him and smack him around just for being there. I was only about five years old and they treated him like this since I was born, so I started doing the same thing.

He would sometimes live with her for a year or two but had to come back because when she moved to a new apartment, they didn't allow dogs. I always wondered why she never took me to live with her, but she always said that he was there before me, so... Plus he only needed to be walked twice a day and I needed 24 hour care. She said he was more independent than me so he could come and I had to stay. She couldn't just leave me in the house like she could with him.

"Well, I can't just leave you in the house by yourself. I ain't going to jail cuz of you".

I really didn't know what to say to that. I was six.

I didn't know it was wrong. They treated him like he wasn't even living and I, not knowing any better, joined them.

My mother didn't see any of this, but sometimes she would come home from work and find him bleeding from the anus or he just wouldn't get up because he was sore.

My mother moved out cause her mother tried to charge her rent and her brothers.

"Why I have to pay rent when they don't get to?".

"Cuz they boys and you got that baby".

"He got a baby too".

"Yea, but you know he ain't takin' care of her like that".

"Well, why I got to pay you rent? I rather pay a real landlord".

That's more or less how it went.

She was off on Sundays and Mondays, but she always came to my grandmother's house to spend time with me, even on days she worked. My grandmother raised me, so a lot of the things I believed in as a child were the same as her.

She quit school during the Great Depression and used to joke all the time about how she went to the 7th grade and my grandfather only went to the 6th so she was smarter.

43

She wanted to be a mapmaker and travel the country. She thought it was such an interesting job to have all that freedom and to see Chicago. She knew about the dangers of traveling the country as a black woman, but she didn't let that stop her from dreaming about it.

She was very religious and sometimes she wouldn't even kick the dog, but she would push him out of the way. She wouldn't abuse him like the others, but she didn't stop it, which some would see as just as bad.

When he passed away, I was shocked. He did find out later that he was elderly and dying of cancer. It just didn't help that they were also beating him.

My mother wanted him to die at home in peace, but she didn't know what was going on. I felt partly responsible for his death and for everything that happened to him. I guess I didn't think he had feelings, maybe because he was an animal. I don't know, I just followed what I saw other people in the house doing and I have guilt over that to this day. It has always been hard for me to be around animals since then. Whether it was the zoo, an animal shelter, or any pets, it's not because I don't like animals, which is what my kids always assumed because I never wanted them to have any pets. It's weird to think animals are always prone to me and I don't know why. I see myself as a bad person with animals. I always felt like I would hurt them by accident and I can't bear to feel like I caused another animal's suffering.

I never even told another person about this experience. I was so ashamed of what I did, I just knew people would look at me differently. It didn't matter that I was so young. I always felt like somehow I should have known better. But even telling this to my daughter now and talking to God I realize it wasn't my fault, it was what I was taught, and I had no one around me at the time to tell me that it was wrong, and being almost 50 now I have to forgive myself.

Shep died from cancer in the house when I was about 8 years old. He died right in front of the bathroom. My grandmother wrapped him up in an old quilt in the closet and dragged him out at about 6 pm where the garbage bags were usually piled up for pick up the next morning. When my mother came by as she did every day after work, she asked my grandmother where Shep was.

Without a word, she pointed up the block to the garbage bags. I will never forget the look on my mother's face when my grandmother pointed to the garbage bags outside the kitchen window. She looked like her heart had just leapt out of her chest. She lost the only friend she had. I looked out the window at that sad blanket holding my mother's dog, someone she loved even more than me.

When I heard the front door slam and saw my mom run up the block and kneel in a mountain of garbage bags in front of the old quilt crying with her head on the quilt screaming to no end, it was the saddest thing I ever saw. My grandmother asked what my mom was doing while she casually doing the dishes. I told her what I saw. My grandmother put down the dishes and came over next to me to see my mother out the window. She shook her head and said, "Look at that fool on the ground fussing over a dog".

Then she just went back to doing dishes. When my mother came back in, they had some words.

"Why you didn't call me and tell me that he died?".

"What you gonna do? You can't do anything about it. What you gonna do bury the dog in the projects?".

My mouth dropped. I was like, wow that's cold.

"You're cruel, how could you?".

"Well, if you felt like that you should have taken him with you".

After that, my mother got in her car and left. She didn't ask me if I was alright or even if I understand about death. I was sad I did miss him and didn't really understand anything that happened that day. She went home, my grandmother continued doing dishes, and I went to bed.

I didn't think my mother was a fool, but as a child, I was shocked at how she went overboard for her dog and didn't shed one tear when her father died 3 years earlier. I cry when I think of Shep now, but then I just felt confused, but sad for my mother. I felt some resentment for Shep because I knew she loved him more than me. I never wanted anything to happen to him and I feel bad that he died, but at the same time I looked at my mother differently because of that. My mother never got a pet after Shep and refused to let any of her children to have any. She said she couldn't bear it again.

11

Chapter 11

Dear Daughter,

In 1980, I was 6 years old and when I got back to New York; it was my time to begin the first grade. I was still in the same school. The one everybody in the projects went to because it was my zone school cuz I lived with my grandmother. I was so excited I thought it was going to be just like kindergarten. I couldn't wait to go to school. The first couple of weeks there, the teacher was mean. I didn't like her at all. I don't remember her name.

I just know she was a mean lady. I remember I asked her if I could go to the bathroom. She said no, so I sat in the back of the class in the middle and I peed right there on myself. After that, when I said I had to go to the bathroom, she let me go cuz she knew I meant it.

One day, I asked if I could go to the bathroom and she gave me the little wooden pass that they had. It was rectangular and hard, it just said pass on one side and girls on the other. When I got to the bathroom, there were a bunch of fifth and sixth graders in there making a lot of noise. They were just pretending to use the bathroom, but they were playing with the water and talking junk.

I used the bathroom and washed my hands. When I turned to go back to class, one girl told me to pull my pants down.

I said, "No. Excuse me, I have to get back to class".

Mind you, I'm only six. It wasn't hard for them to grab me and push me back into the stall. I kept fighting them and tried my best to get to the bathroom door. I just needed to escape.

I didn't know what they wanted to do to me, but I was so frightened. I managed to grab the silver handle of the bathroom stall.

I thought I could make it out, but then one girl stabbed me with a sharp pencil in my hand. It hurt, but I didn't give up and somehow I made it out of the bathroom. I cried as I ran straight to my teacher and I told her everything that had happened. She took me to the office and then called my mother. My mother came to the school livid.

My mother took me home and I think I left my books at the school. I know the next day she took me to the board of Education to complain about what happened.

The complaint had to take time, so I still had to complete the week in that school.

Teachers were allowed to hit kids in school and when your table is bad, you all of you aren't allowed to talk during lunch. If they did, then all the kids at that table had to stand up and get smacked on the hand a few times with a ruler. I remember her saying, "better be glad you're not going on that stage".

I didn't know what that meant until there was a Friday assembly.

It was so strange. All these kids from kindergarten to six grade would line up on the stage and expose their ass and spank them with a ruler in front of the entire school. I just knew I needed to get out of that school.

I don't know if I skipped first grade. I believe I did cuz when I started my new school I was in the second grade. During that first year that I was home before I started second grade, I watched a lot of Sesame Street. I guess I learned a lot from Sesame Street, enough that could skip a grade.

I guess it took a long time for the paperwork to go through, cuz until everything was settled, I was home-schooled. Uncle James was the one who mainly taught me, which I still appreciate. He did have the help of channel 13 and I still went to church.

He taught me how to use an abacus. Even though back then we called it a Chinese calculator. It was my first calculator. I still have it to this day. Don't laugh at me. It wasn't the Flintstones, but we didn't have computers. We would have an assembly in school just to see a computer be turned on. It was crazy. It didn't have a mouse. That came later, but you could use the ball to move the cursor around. It was like the size of a pool ball that sat on a stand. The arrow would be flying all over the place, which is why they created the mouse, I guess.

Y'all all fancy now with the mouse and shit. We didn't have the click features. If you fucked up, you had to write that bitch all over.

I don't fuck with the touch screen laptops, it's voodoo.

Stop fuckin laughin' at me.

49

12

Chapter 12

Dear Daughter,

After that, I started having some awful nightmares and started to pee in the bed every night. My grandmother thought it was because I used to drink water before I went to bed. It wasn't that. I knew I had to go to the bathroom. I was just too scared to go. It was dark and the only light they kept on in the house was in the kitchen and bathroom.

Every time I got up to go to the bathroom, no word of a lie, I saw two enormous dogs that were standing in the doorway, growling and snarling at me. Like Cerberus standing at the gates of the Underworld or Fenrir waiting for the start of Ragnarok. They had big piercing red eyes that seemed never to blink. They didn't have back legs. It was like smoke seeping from the back that led into the ground. They looked like big mutts. I couldn't move. I was paralyzed.

I would try to go back to bed, but then it felt like someone was holding the door and it wouldn't budge. Like someone was trying to keep me there. I was trapped and panic would envelop me. To my family, it was one big joke that I couldn't make it to the bathroom at night, but I was terrified to go to bed. Knowing that those dogs would appear from the depths of Hell to intimidate and terrorize me.

I told my grandmother; she said it was a dream but I know what I saw. I was told that if the hounds of Hell were after you; you had to pray them away. So I prayed. I went to church with my grandmother and sometimes she used to catch me in my room on a Saturday or after church on a Sunday and I had all my dolls lined up on the floor. I would pretend I was the pastor and I read from a kid's Bible that I had.

When my grandmother found me playing church, she beat me and told me I was making fun of God and that women couldn't be pastors.

That was the first and last time I played church.

My grandmother had a family bible. You know, the really big one with the entire family tree in it. I didn't learn how to read it till I got older, but I still love looking at the pictures.

The picture that stuck with me the most was the picture of Daniel and the Lion's Den. I don't know if anyone remembers that story, but I remember that picture clearly. He had a robe. I believe it was navy blue, and he was looking out the window of a jail cell with his arms behind his back. They threw him in the den of lions and they wanted the Lions to eat him. He was looking out the window and he believed in God and a lion was behind him the whole time, but they never attacked. It just stared at him and he stared out the window at God.

That picture resonates with me to this day. I don't know why, but I kept praying and the more I prayed and the more I went to church, the dogs seemed like they got closer and meaner every time.

My grandmother put the 23 psalm under my pillow and it did help. I still had nightmares, but the dogs left. There were there for years until I was twelve. They kept telling me to pray, but no one taught me how to pray. I learned how to play from Little house on the prairie.

I was always tired of going to school, but it was cuz I couldn't sleep. I was scared as shit.

13

Chapter 13

Dear Daughter,

Once my mother bought me a bike. I was so excited, and it had training wheels, but I was still excited. No kid wants to have training wheels even if they know they can't ride a bike.

It was a black bike with red fire on the side. It was beautiful. She got one of the neighborhood kids to teach me how to ride. I fell a couple of times with the training wheels on. One day I said, "I'm going to take these training wheels off".

One kid in the neighborhood took the training wheels off so I could learn how to balance. I probably should have kept the training wheel so I could learn that way first before I took them off, but I knew I could learn without them.

I was riding fine with the training wheels at first. Going straight was fine, but when I went to turn the corner, I fell. There used to always be crack rocks and broken glass bottles all over the place. It was the 80s. So, of course, I fell into a pile of glass. I bust my lip and the kid brought me to the house. It was around noon and the kid told my mother that I fell and hurt myself.

My mother took me to the bathroom, put ice in a washcloth, and placed it on my lip so the swelling could go down.   I apologized for falling and she said it was fine cuz everybody falls.

Then she said, "I see you are never going to learn how to ride a bike".

"No, I will".

She ignored me no matter how much I told her that I just needed a little more time. Her mind was set, and there was no way I could convince her. I just figured that I could show her by trying really hard and I would get there soon.

The next day, she sold my bike to someone in the neighborhood. It broke my heart. To think that my mother believed in my failure more than even giving me a chance to overcome this obstacle. Riding a bike is a milestone in any child's life. It's in the hallmark movies and everything. Teaching your child how to ride their bike and show them to never give up. When you fall, you just brush yourself off and try again. Not my mother. Her lesson was to never tell her anything, or I was sure to fail. If I was going to achieve anything, she would have to find out after the fact. She was always great at making people feel small and incapable.

My Uncle Buddy found out what happened and sent me Barbie skates from West Virginia. I fell many times on the skates, but I never told my mother. I was scared she was going to sell my skates, and they were fish-a-price skates. By the end of the summer, I mastered the skates.

My mother didn't know it took me more than one day to learn how to use them. It took me about 2 weeks but I knew not to tell her. I learned my lesson.

The neighborhood kids tried to teach me how to ride on their bikes but when my mother caught me, oh, she used to scream. She used to beat me to get off those kids' bikes.

"I ain't got no money to buy them no bike. Stop taking people's stuff," she would say. I guess she just thought I was so bad that I would break their bikes if I even touched them. It was that, or she didn't want to be wrong. If she said something, she hated to be wrong, even if it was something bad.

The kids in the neighborhood tried to teach me cuz they knew what my mother did and they felt bad for me. It was so bad that when they used to try to teach me; she used to go to their parents and their parents threatened to ground them. They were still allowed to play with me and talk with me, but they never put me on a bike again. To this day, I still don't know how to ride a bike. All four of my children learned how to ride a bike and even offered to teach me, but I don't want to. I do want a three wheeled bike though.

I think they are so cute. I want a pink one with a basket on it. I know I'll get one someday and I can't wait. I don't give a fuck. And I want my tiny dog Lavender sitting in the basket in the front.

I do still love to skate and I did teach y'all well. All of you are very fast learners and even when it did take a bit longer for you guys to learn, I never told you that you couldn't do it even when you wanted to quit. I tried to instill in my all my children that you can do anything you wanted to do and anything you thought you couldn't do. You shouldn't limit yourself for any reason and when people tell you, you can't do something. All you had to do was prove them wrong.

It's hard to teach kids these lessons from them putting their pride in front of what is right and wrong. Peer pressure is a real thing that I learned the hard way as well and didn't want any of my kids falling for that same trap.

Just cuz someone tells you, you can't do something doesn't mean to do it, but if it is something you fell passionate about and it is a positive thing that don't hurt anyone that was when you should put in the work and achieve it. They achieved more than I could imagine.

14

Chapter 14

Dear Daughter,

After my grandfather died everything, just seemed to get worse. The attack in school, the dogs I used to see, me peeing in the bed at night. I was only six; it was so bad, and I wanted my grandfather so much.

I was in so much pain and I kept reading the Bible and I kept asking God why was all this happening to me. I'm only a little girl. I just didn't feel like it was going to get better. People called me names. I know I wasn't the most attractive little girl. I wish I didn't hear them when I was playing with my friends. Other than calling me pockets, they called me ugly.

Saying things like "Oh, I hope she looks better when she gets older. I hope fine somebody".

This wasn't even from the other kids like you would expect. It was mainly from the adults, including my mother. Instead of her defending me, she agreed with them. She felt like it was better coming from her than a stranger. That it was better for her to put me down first before other people could do it. I still don't understand that logic, but she just says I don't understand. I don't, but whatever.

I just felt like I wasn't enough. I didn't understand what was wrong with me.

I would try to convince myself that everything was alright. Just telling myself that I was fine and that everything would be okay. I went to church and God says you are supposed to love everyone and treat everyone with kindness. I just didn't understand why I didn't get that same love, but going to church I realized that heaven was wonderful and beautiful and everyone's always happy. No one's ever judging you or looking at you like you're in the way. God loves everyone and there are angels and everyone flies.

To me, it was a magical place, and I was like "I wanted to go there". I used to think that my grandfather was there and he'll take care of me like he always did. I don't think my grandmother believed he went there, but I would just ignore those comments.

1980 was the year of my first attempt at suicide at the age of 6 years old. From what I understand, I don't remember now. I just remember being in the hospital, but then the rest is a blur. I think I put Lysol or bleach, some cleaning solution. I believe in my oatmeal or cereal. That's what the family said. The next thing I knew, instead of my family talking to me and asking me what was wrong, my mother signed me up for therapy in the neighborhood. She said needed someone to talk to, to figure out what was wrong with me.

It looked like a help center. It was nice. I remember the man's name, my first therapist, Mr. Stanley Griffith. He looked like a young Billy D. Williams. I was so shy I didn't understand why I was there. I remember him having puppets and dolls in his room. I was very comfortable with him. I sat with him in his office and would play with the dolls. I went every week. The first two weeks I didn't say a word but the third week he said "So are you ready to talk to me now?".

I let him know what was going on cuz every adult in my life by that time was cruel. Besides my kindergarten teacher, my grandfather, my aunt, and my uncle. It was rare for an adult to ask me how I was doing and mean it. I wanted to talk to him. It was the first time I felt truly heard.

He asked me if I remembered the incident and I said no. He asked me why I did what I did. I told him that I wanted to be with my grandfather and God.

He was taking notes and said "Would you like to play for a little while". It was an hour-long session, and I had 15 minutes left. It was nice to have someone to play with. I was an only child, so there wasn't much I wanted to talk about, and doing this made me feel comfortable with him. We would play Connect Four, puppets, and they had a little kitchen set.

We would have tea parties, it was nice. After that, I couldn't wait to go see him. We still talked, but he played and talked and sometimes if I didn't feel like talking, if I just wanted to play, he let me play. He was so nice to me. I went to therapy for years, but only had two therapists. I had to change therapist eventually cuz he said that I was becoming a young lady and should talk to a woman. If I had a choice, I would have stayed with him. I guess it was deemed inappropriate at the time if I stayed with him.

After years of going to therapy, I didn't like therapy cause I was forced to go. I never wanted you guys to go to therapy because of how I felt when I was going when I was a teenager. I know now that therapy can help and many people benefit from going, but it took me a long time to understand this. It was always assumed that people who go to therapy were crazy and needed help. I didn't want to be called crazy or anything like that. Therapy did help me as a child, but it also came with a stigma that I didn't want my children to deal with.

15

Chapter 15

Dear Daughter,

When I went to second grade, I was seven, and I had my first birthday party since I was one. I did know that usually, people had a birthday party every year, but not me. Most people in my family don't have a party every year, but they would celebrate. I didn't celebrate my birthday at all.

It was a Snow White and the Seven Dwarfs party. All my cousins came to celebrate with me and my cake was beautiful. It even had all the seven dwarfs on it. I was so excited. I still have the picture, it was so much fun. Snow White was the first Disney cartoon I ever saw, and I fell in love instantly. I didn't get any gifts other than clothes and money, but they gave them to my mother so I didn't get anything for me. My mother didn't give me anything.

I asked, "Do I have a gift?".

She told me, "You should be happy you got a party. Don't be ungrateful, that's why I don't get you anything".

She planned no more parties for me cause she told me that I

was born in the winter and who was going to come. I was told that I was born at the wrong time. I don't know how that was my fault, but I wasn't going to tell her that.

My Aunt Bunny always sent me money, but I didn't know that till I was a teen cause my mother would take the money. I only found out cuz my grandmother checked the mail. That's when she started giving it directly to me. I went to other people's parties, but I was used to not having one. I know it sounds sad, but I got used to it. She would get me a cake every year, but it was either pineapple or carrot cake with raisins. When I told her I didn't like those flavors, she said to be grateful, and that she was buying it. It was her favorite cake, so she got it for my birthday every single year.

When she gave me my first gift, I was sixteen, and I thanked her, but I was surprised. She said that she felt like getting me something cause I was sixteen now. I didn't ask how that made any sense cuz it still doesn't, but I knew better than to question my mother when something told her to be nice. Why look a gift horse in the mouth, especially when it's so rare? It's like asking a unicorn why it exists. It simply doesn't matter.

16

Chapter 16

Dear Daughter,

When I went to second grade, I was a little nervous, but Mr. Griffith told me everything was going to be okay, and I believed it. So, when I started going to school in Forest Hills, it was strange because the students were predominantly white. There's nothing wrong with white people. It was just the most I've ever seen. The school that I went to before was predominantly black.

I had to take the yellow school bus there and back. My second-grade teacher was Miss Duran. She was a very thin white lady with glasses. I remember her to be very sweet to me.

The best part of my new school was that my aunt, my grandmother's sister, worked there as a teacher's aide. She assisted the lunchroom office or whenever they needed her. I know she was an aide. That's all I know. It was nice to see her during recess at lunchtime now and then. To have someone I knew would look out for me was a comfort, especially with what happened at my last school. Everyone respected her in the school and was like everyone's aunt. It was just convenient for me that she was my family.

In the middle of my second-grade year, there was a guy on the bus named Robert. I don't know why, but every day on the way to school and on the way home he would steal my hat and play keep away with it. I don't know if someone has ever played keep away with anything of yours, but it is a stereotypical bullying tactic. Even with how childish and immature it is, it is one of the most frustrating and dehumanizing things someone can do to you. For me to have an older kid do that to me every day for a year, for no reason, was annoying. There are brief words that can be said about how helpless I felt on that bus. I lived too far away to avoid it. I did have cousins who also went to this school with me and were on the bus, but I was the oldest, so it wasn't like they could have helped much, even if they wanted to.

He used to take my hat, then call me Ugly and ask why I was on his bus. Like he had some sort of ownership over how people went to school. Like my presence personally offended him. How could I dare to be on the bus and look the way I did? It wasn't like I cared much about what he called me because it wasn't like I hadn't heard it before from my family or the people in my neighborhood. I became numb to those types of insults.

"I thought dogs walk, they Don't Ride".

In the third grade, I had Miss Phoenix. She was my first black teacher since kindergarten. Her mother lived in the nursing home where my mother worked. So my mother knew almost everything about me that year. My reading was good, my math not so much. They had something called the resource room, where Miss Wilcox would take a bunch of kids into the library and have a projector propped up on a book and speed read. She would ask how many words we could read in five minutes. It was some type of test that I still don't quite understand. She also helped us with math. I was better at reading, though.

I learned how to become a strong reader. By the end of that year, I loved the library. Once a week they'll have the class go to the library. I would get any book I could get my hands on and if the book was too hard for me, I would ask someone to read it to me. I'd try to figure out the words and not look at the pictures. I still love to read even though I read about three or four books at once. If I get bored with one, I read the other and get back to it when I feel like it.

My grandmother used to take me to the movies. My father's mother loved to go to the movies. Whether it was always appropriate, what we were watching is debatable. I remember when Annie came out, and I wanted to see it so badly. I asked her over and over if we could go see it in the theaters. Of course, she said no.

"We're gonna see whatever I want to see and if you don't like it, you don't have to go. I don't like stupid pictures".

She took me to see Death Wish 4 with Charles Bronson. Oh my God, it was inappropriate. I had nightmares for a week. The fight scenes were good, but there was a lot of sex in it. Watching it, it was violent. I wasn't aroused, I should say, but I felt a little weird, like it awakened something in me. Like sexually. Then I felt ashamed of it and I felt like I had to pray. I was so small, and no one explained to me anything that was going on. Suddenly I knew what sex was, but I didn't at the same time. I just felt so uncomfortable feeling all these feelings and not knowing why or how to deal with them. I was too young to be exposed to everything in this movie.

I did end up going to see Annie with my mother, her friend, and a couple of kids in the neighborhood. My mother thought

I went to see Annie with my grandmother, but I didn't. My grandmother told me to promise not to tell my mother that we went to go see Death Wish 4. I was very good with secrets, especially with family.

I'm good with secrets now. It's mainly because when people tell me secrets, I usually forget what they told me. So, I saw Annie for the first time. It was great. I still love Annie and I mean any version of it, really. There's just something about watching a young, strong-willed girl go from running away and living in a terrible home and ending up having a loving family, even if it wasn't the one she thought she would have. Sometimes things don't always happen the way you want them to, but that doesn't mean it's not good enough.

17

Chapter 17

Dear Daughter,

My cousin used to fight a lot with the kids in the neighborhood. Not so much fist fight, more like start arguments. By this time, her mom passed away, and she was living with us full time. I don't know why, but everybody would be playing outside and the next thing you know, she's fighting with someone and I would jump in. I would turn around and she's in the house.

My mother used to say, "If you go fight for her again, I'm going to beat you for protecting her. She leave you out here fighting your battles and she in the house".

But I thought that's what you're supposed to do for family. It was fucked up cuz I was standing there fighting my friends for her.

She was my little cousin, and she didn't have a big sister. I thought it was up to me to take on the role.

I didn't realize at the time that I didn't have to. I had no obligation to fight her battles, especially when she never fought herself.

I felt somebody had to protect her, and I thought that someone had to be me. Nobody protected me, but I was determined to protect her.

We were so close that my mother took us both to Disney World once on a church trip. My cousin would always come on trips with us for family vacations, even when her father never took me anywhere. Even when we went to Disney World, her father didn't chip in anything for her. My mother paid for her and never asked for anything from her brother.

Going to Disney World for the first time was amazing. I loved to go to Magic Kingdom, it's still my favorite place in Disney World. To see the castle and all the princess stuff. I like rides, but I always loved feeling like a princess. Everything pink and sparkly always got my attention. We only spent one day at Disney World, but I loved it. I didn't even know there were other parks in Disney World until I got older. I found out when I was older that we had a choice on what parks to go to and she choose Magic Kingdom cuz we were little girls and Sea World.

My mother loved aquariums, which I really don't care for. I don't see the point of looking at fish. They don't do much, anyway. We sat there and watched fish flip; I was so mad when I found out we didn't have to go there. It was before there were even rides there. Again, I never really liked looking at animals or being near animals, but I thought sea creatures were just boring to look at and not a fun, boring, a dull type of boring.

Me and my cousin did a lot of stuff together, like playing in the park. Especially at the enormous park away from home. There was an enormous park that had a giant playground that we would play at cuz my mother was on the softball team. So on Saturdays she had to play games and we would go watch.

She had a great arm. She was a pitcher and played shortstop.

She was very athletic back then. I didn't play softball, but I did run track and play basketball and volleyball when I was in high school. I did go to a tryout for softball, but when they threw the ball at me, I blacked out.

The ball didn't hit me, but it did go past me and I was like "Nope, not for me".

I left class and went straight to my guidance counselor to change classes.

I put you guys in sports at a very young age and you went whether you liked it or not. I felt like it was better for you to be there than to be on the street or sitting at home. Y'all liked going outside anyway, so this gave some structure with all that time.

Me and my cousin used to play and get ice cream from the truck. We used to do everything together, but when we got around other members of our extended family, they started comparing me to her. We never noticed the difference between each other until others pointed it out.

She was light-skinned, and I was brown skinned. There was a little girl across the hall and we were friends, but when my cousin came around, I was pushed to the side and at the time I didn't know why. We used to have slumber parties and stay the night and have fun and play little tricks on each other.

But I felt like Rudolph, and I wasn't allowed to play in the reindeer games. They didn't play tricks on me and I know some people would be happy that they didn't get tricks played on them, but I wanted to be included in all the activities, good or bad.

Sometimes the little girl would have slumber parties and they wouldn't invite me if my cousin wasn't there. Mind you, they did live across the hall from me and I would find out the next day or so, but if my cousin went and spent a weekend with her mother, I wouldn't be able to go. At this time, I was seven and didn't understand what was really happening. I just knew I wanted to be included, and I was being left out.

I would be confused when other girls in the neighborhood wanted to play with her and not me. Mind you, I knew the girls first, but suddenly they didn't want to play with me. I didn't care. I would just tell her that I was going to play with the older girls.

I just thought it was strange. I didn't really understand color-ism. It's hard to comprehend color-ism or any form of racism without being explained what it is. I was just experiencing it. I didn't know what it was called, or that it was a thing in general. I just knew that it didn't feel good.

I didn't blame her for how we were being treated and I figured she was fine cause she wasn't being left out. I don't claim to know what she thought at the time or even what she thinks about it now. She was like a little sister to me and if it wasn't for our childhood, maybe we would have stayed friends like we were in the beginning.

My mother thought that I was a fool because if people didn't play with my cousin, I would refuse to play too. I would sit with her on the bench and wait until they decided that she could play, but when kids wanted to play with her and not me, she would go with them saying, "They only want to play with me".

I noticed a difference when we went to school, too. When people asked if we were cousins, she wouldn't deny me, but she would deny our other cousins that went to the school cuz she said they were unattractive. She said she couldn't deny me because everyone already knew that we lived together.

She would look at me like she felt bad for me or something,

but would never say anything.

Even though our parents are twins, it's not like what you see in the movies where the twins are inseparable. They have always had a complex relationship of jealousy and petty rivalries. They tried to keep it away from me and my cousin, but it only resulted in her being invited to everything and me not being invited to anything.

They still have a strange relationship and by that I mean not really at all.

They are barely in the same room and know very little about color-ism lives and what they do know is usually talk they hear from other people in the family. The family has never been the type of people to hold in what they think about someone, and when they are siblings, there is no filter. They don't even really have the excuse of respecting their elders, since they are twins a few minutes can only mean so much and to them, it means nothing.

18

Chapter 18

Dear Daughter,

I kept going to West Virginia in the Summers, doing the same things like fishing, picnicking, learn how to swim. I was in the third grade. It was great it took me all summer, but I came back an average swimmer.

Now the fourth grade was very tough. I still had to go to school on the bus, but by this time, another person joined the festivities of my torture. I never forget about Tanya. It was weird cuz I was best friends with her sister, Kenya.

There were three of us: me, Felicia, and Kenya. Me and Felicia stopped being friend during junior high, cuz she joined the cool kids like a stereotypical teen movie. She ended up getting killed by her baby daddy around the end of high school. They were fighting over child support and he shot her twice in the chest and kidnapped her daughter. It was all over the news. He was a correction officer, so it much has been a hell of an argument. Her daughter was found safe, and he went to prison. I didn't go to the funeral, but we hadn't been friends for years and she left me for the popular kids. I don't feel like I owed her anything.

She had no hair, glasses, and was really skinny. It was her and her sister after their mom died and their father was taking care of them. He tried his best, but he didn't know how to take care of girls. Kenya just ended up being shy and Tanya was angry. They were kind of homely, but she didn't like me.

While Robert was played keep away with my hat. I was still scared of what Robert felt like he wanted to do to me that day, whether that was going to school or on the way home.

By this time, I was getting sick and tired of the harassment and random abuse. I decided that I would go to the back of the bus. The high would sit in the front and the sixth graders would sit in the back of the bus.

Because I was in the fourth grade, I felt like I was old enough and strong enough to stand up for myself. So I was going to go to stand up to Robert and get my hat.

Boy, what a mistake that was. I tried to do the Daniel in the lion's den and stand up for myself, but I guess I should have called God first. Maybe he was busy. Maybe it only works with people and animals.

The new testament God is nice, but I needed that old testament Lord.

Tanya grabbed me, choked me and beat me up in the aisle of the bus. And you know how tight the aisle of the bus is, so there was nowhere to go. Mind you, my cousin was present for all the beatings, but she ignored me and looked out the window.

I don't know if she wanted to help, but was afraid.

This happened every year until I got to the sixth grade when they finally graduated and I was in the back of the bus. I was so happy I could have bought her flowers. I as so happy I made it.

After that attack in fourth grade, I started pretending to be sick sometimes. I didn't want to leave the house. I especially didn't want to get on the bus.

I thought I was old enough to fight back, but they were older than me and would always be older than me. They were stronger and faster than I was.

I would say I had chicken pocks, measles or the mumps. You know the regular kid's illnesses. I did get all those illnesses as a child cuz people weren't getting vaccinated then. That's why when I had each of y'all I made sure you all got their immunizations as soon as possible, so you wouldn't have to deal with that.

I did pretend to be sick a lot cuz I didn't want to go to school. I just wanted to stay in bed with my dolls and cry and pray and wait for the summer to come.

I would sit in bed and try to read, but if it was anything other than the Bible, then my grandmother would say, "I thought you were sick".

I would try to hide other books in the Bible. I was allowed to watch TV, though. My house was weird.

I didn't know it then, but I realize that I was depressed. I didn't know that kids could be depressed.

In school other kids would ask me "why are you so ugly?".

"I don't know. Blame my parents. How you blaming me for how I look, like I chose to look this way?".

To me, I thought I was fine. Obviously, I wasn't in their eyes.

19

Chapter 19

Dear Daughter,

That fourth grade year in the middle of the school year, I was sitting in class and I had to go to the bathroom.

No... I'm wrong. I got up to go to the board cuz the teacher called me to do a math problem. I believe I did it the best I could. I was going back to my seat all the way in the back when the boy who sat next to me said "Deneque".

I said "yes".

"Did you cut yourself?".

"No, why?".

"You're bleeding in the back".

"What do you mean, I'm bleeding?"

I raised my hand and asked if I could go to the bathroom. The teacher gave me the wooden pass, and I started searching the halls, looking for my aunt.

"I know she's down here somewhere". She had a little office, but she wasn't there. As a last resort, I went to the security guard that would sit near the front door.

Mr Wiggins was a mean man, an asshole, a real asshole. I told him that I needed my aunt and that it was an emergency. He pulled out his walkie-talkie and did his thing. Next thing you know, my aunt comes down the hall.

I told her what happened, so she took me to her little office and gave me a maxi pad. They didn't have wings, they only had the ones that stick, but they didn't have that kind in school. It was a small box and the maxi pad was about as long as my forearm.

She safety penned it onto my panties and told me to sit right there. She grabbed me a pair of pants out of the lost and found to put on.

She went to my teacher, told her what happened and drove me home in the middle of the day.

My grandmother was like "Oh my goodness".

My stomach started to hurt and my grandmother made me some tea, but I threw it up right away. I had diarrhea and my grandmother gave me another pad similar to the one my aunt gave me at school. She taught me how to change it.

Mind you, I'm only nine years old. My grandmother was trying to be maternal, but wasn't the brightest bulb.

So, she called my mother, who was at work, saying "Oh, now she can get pregnant".

She then turned to me saying, "Don't kiss no one cuz you get pregnant. Keep your skirt down now, you got to be careful".

"Now you got to watch her," she told my mother.

Keep in my, no one at this point has told me what has happened. So, all I know is that if I kiss someone, I will get pregnant and that I have to be careful of what I do. I don't know anything about sex at this point or what a period means for me. I didn't know that it was called a period until I was twelve.

I would try to ask my friends if they bleed and they said bleed where. I thought I was a freak. My aunt was sweet and gave me a hug and told me congratulations.

I told my therapist, and he asked if anyone talked to me about being a woman and I told him I'm not a woman. I found out later that he spoke to my mother about talking to me, but she said what am I supposed to say? This is what I pay you for. He felt uncomfortable cause he was a man, so i didn't get that talk.

Bunny and Buddy just told me that I was a woman now, but still didn't tell me what that meant. I just wanted someone to explain it to me.

"It happens," my mother said.

"What happened?".

It was always just "she got it".

"How long does it last?".

I was so confused and there was so much blood that I thought I was going to die. My mind was everywhere, I couldn't handle it. I was like, oh my God, I'm too young to be a mother. I didn't know anything about babies. And the pain just kept coming. It was painful. Oh, my God. I thought I was dying. I thought it just came maybe once a year, but then I found out that it came out every month.

It used to be so heavy that I used to take so many pills, Tylenol, Motrin whatever take hot water bottles and put it on my stomach. I would put a pillow between my legs. I just kept throw up and having diarrhea. Every month I did get to stay home. It was not like I liked my period, but it did give me a break from the school bus.

I didn't have to be tortured in two ways. I told my mother about the beating and such, but she told me to ignore them.

I don't know how I could ignore being choked and smacked

and punched, etc.

She then had my aunt deal with it at school since she worked there, but that just made them beat me up more because I snitched. After a while, I just started making up lies about why I kept coming home with bruises and such. Saying things like I fell on the playground.

My mother would just say, "If you don't know how to play, you should stay off those swings". She says that I have always been clumsy. She still says that I clumsy, even though I was just getting fucked up. It wasn't an accident.

I did tell my therapist, and he told me to tell my mother. He would ask why they did it and I told him that it was because they thought I was ugly. He asked if that was it and it was. When I did blame my parents for my looks, the other kids just laughed at me and still kicked my ass so...

When I was young, I asked my parents why they didn't sleep with other people because maybe I would have turned out different. I didn't understand that. That's not how that works. I blamed my parents for sleeping with each other and creating someone as ugly as me.

I asked my father, "Am I ugly?".

His response was, "Hopefully you'll look better when you get older".

I know now that that's not the way I should have been thinking, but I didn't know how else to feel. Not many people at the time were telling me I was beautiful. Even my family thought I was ugly.

My grandmother used to walk us to the bus stop every day and picked us up till we got in about sixth grade. By the time I was about twelve where I could walk home by myself.

The bus stop wasn't too far from where we lived, but it was

the 80s. For some reason, she used to walk us to the bus stop for school, but at the age of nine, I was still able to walk to the store by myself. I wasn't able to cross the street without help, I guess, so my grandmother used to look out the window and see if any cars were coming around the corner. It was a one way so she would have me wait at the corner and yell from the window when it was safe for me to cross.

I think it's common knowledge in the 80s things were terrible. There were certain gangs that was were dying down, but others were coming up. The music was getting good cuz that when hip hop was coming out. Drive-by shootings started to be popular. Even annual block parties got canceled cuz of shoot outs..

There was crack everywhere. Drugs were easy to get and used by many. Plus, there was HIV, but no one knew how you got it. We thought you could get it from a hand shaker. Maybe it was airborne. We didn't know.

Especially in New York City, it was bad. People were snatching kids, and it was just a weird time for everyone.

We actually had a guy who used to drive around in a van named Diaper Man. He set up in a van under a little bridge up the block from my house and just watched kids go to the store.

He literally would open up the side door of his van and know you. He kept track of the children who would walk by themselves and those who were with their parents. To lore children into his van, he used a single piece of candy places delicately in the palm of his open hand. I can still see the pinks of his palms attached to a middle-aged white hand. His face was never visual, or maybe I don't remember it. Maybe I just wasn't looking. I was young and terrified. He didn't say a word and would just wait to see who took the bait.

The next thing you know, kids were found on the railroad

tracks. It was horrifying.

All I could think was that it easily could have been me. If I took the candy or if he was feeling bold that day, he could have easily overpowered me. I wasn't a big girl or very strong. It would have been easy for him and I know I wouldn't have had a chance against him.

I would tell my mother that I didn't want to go to the store by myself, but all she would say is, "No one wants you. Go to the store".

I don't know what she was thinking, honestly. I wonder if a serial killer wouldn't take a child cuz they thought they were ugly. Not really something people usually talk about. In that case, I guess my looks helped me? I don't know.

One day when I was going to the store I saw his van under the bridge. He opened the van, and all you saw was darkness. I was scared and when I turned to my right, there was a short black lady standing there. She asked if I minded if she walked with me. I told I didn't care and took her hand.

"Where did you come from?".

She just smiled at me and said, "I'm just going to the store".

I didn't care. I was just happy that she was there. I wasn't scared of her and it felt like I knew her, but I never seen her before.

"Are you OK?".

"No. I'm scared".

"Of what?".

"The van".

"It's OK, I'm with you".

Then, while we were walking to the store, I asked her, "Do you believe in God?".

"Yes".

"Then where is he?".

She smiled and said, "He's always with you".

She passed and asked, "Do you believe in guardian angels?".

"I don't know. I don't think so".

And then, which I found to be weird, she asked, "Do you think God hears your prayers?".

I said "I don't know. I pray, but I don't get no answers".

"He knows what's happening with you. He sees it".

Then she just explained to me that there was a plan for me and that I was on the right path and that I just need to hang in there. I just thought she was crazy. I didn't know what she was talking about.

Then we reached the store. I got what I needed while she waited outside, then she walked me back. She just kept telling me all the way back how God loves me and that he sees me and is listening. That he has a plan for me and that everything will get better. The whole time she was telling me this, she was just smiling at me. She told me that everything that was happening wasn't my fault.

I felt like she knew what I was going through, even though I didn't tell her.

After we got past the van and we reached the driveway of the church right behind the projects, she was gone. I don't know where she went. She just disappeared.

For the next two weeks, I was still sent to the store, and each time she would show up and walk with me. She never bought anything, and she never went inside. She just kept telling me that I was meant to be her and that it way okay.

She did make me feel better. She would tell me that I was special, beautiful, and loved. She told me to keep talking to God, and I told her that I didn't know how to pray. She told me to just talk to him like I would talk to anyone.

I asked her when these things were going to happen and when was things were going to get better. She just smiled at me and told me to trust her and me for some reason, even though I didn't know her that well. I did. The way she looked at me, it was like she saw what I was going to become.

One day, she just disappeared, and I never saw her again.

To this day, I still know that she was my guardian angel. I didn't see it at nine, of course, but I know now.

I know that it might sound a bit clique, but I know that God was listening to me and that all I needed to do was push through.

I don't know if they ever caught him, but there was a string of prostitutes and children that went missing or were found dead from '82 to '84. That's also when his van disappeared and I only see him now in my mind's eye.

Chapter 20

Dear Daughter,

My fourth-grade teacher, Ms. McDougal, was an old short little white lady. She took the class to the planetarium for a field trip, and it was awful. Don't get me wrong, I didn't mind looking at the big dipper and the little dipper, but that day was awful. My mother used to love the planetarium. It just made me dizzy. I also just waited till the end to ask when a shooting star came around. Whether it was every five or ten years. I wanted to make a wish to change my situation.

For lunch I had a pickled pig's foot, a kosher dell pickle, and a quarter water. Do you know bad a pickled pig's foot smells in the heat? My mother felt terrible, but she couldn't afford anything else. It was in a Tupperware container. It was an all white school, and they had never seen a pig's foot before. They were like "Ew, what is that? Is that a toe?".

I was so embarrassed. I remember there was this girl named Micheal who was crying while eating sushi talking about how her father was in Paris with his new girlfriend and her mother was in Japan with her new boyfriend after their divorce. She was being raised by the housekeeper. I was mad at her at the time cuz I was eating pig's foot and she was crying over sushi. Not because she had sushi, mind you, just because of other things going on in her life.

It took me a while to realize that even rich people have problems, but from where I was sitting that day, she didn't have much to cry about. Granted, being an only child was hard for her. The only friends she really had were the staff. I do know that now she is married and has kids. She is a normal person now and, from what I can tell; she is happy. I'm happy for her.

I'm sure now she put her parents in a home or something cuz it's not like they really cared for her like they should have been.

I do feel bad for her now, for all that she went through, and I imagine it was a very sensitive time for her. I just would have been happy not to change lives with her, but to at least have traded lunches that day.

I couldn't wait to get back to the school for the day to be over, but no. I got back to the school and the security guard, Mr. Wiggins, asked, "What you do now?".

I did not like that old motherfucka. He used to always call me an ugly little girl and my reply was, "You're old and you're fat. I hope you die".

Years later, when I heard from my aunt that he died, I laughed for half an hour. He died sad and alone. That's what you get for making fun of children. I know you're not supposed to wish death on people, but I was nine, so...

I appreciate you if you do not laugh while I tell you this story. (Sorry. I'm trying).

Anyway, I said that. I rolled my eyes at him and went with my class down the hall back to the classroom. Before we got back to the classroom, Ms. McDougal took the entire class to the bathroom. The girls in one, the boys in the other. On my way into the bathroom, I saw my mother run out of the office from the corner of my eye.

As you can imagine, I'm thinking, oh God, what is she doing here? She wasn't alone. She was with my aunt and she was trying to calm her down.

I'm like "Aww shit".

She took me into the bathroom, and my aunt followed. Ms. McDougal was confused and asked, "who's this woman?".

"Stay out of it. I'm Deneques mother".

Then she pulled out a big black belt out of her purse. I saw the belt and ran into a stall. Mind you, she didn't have the other girls leave the bathroom, so they stopped doing everything and watched. They only watched for a second, cuz once they saw what was going on and they ran out of the bathrooms and were telling the boys what was going on. They were scared. These were white kids. They never seen someone get beat before. My mother was only twenty-nine, so she was youthful and she chased me.

I'm screaming "what did I do?".

"You got suspended from the bus".

"It wasn't my fault!".

She didn't want to hear it.

I was crawling from one stall to the other. She yanked a door open. I would close it. I would try to move to the other side of the bathroom and she would grab my foot. She's swinging the belt at the same time. She did catch me a few times, more than I would like. The belt is flying, and I was running. The kids were standing around in shock just watching it.

"Imma call the cops", said Ms. McDougal.

85

"Stay out of it. It's family business" is all my aunt said.

I was so mad at Ms. McDougal. Don't just stand there and threaten to call the cops. She should have just called them. Fucking standing there and watching. Call them bitch. Do something Lord, help me. Fuckin empty promises.

She ended up taking the rest of the class down the hall until it was over so the kids didn't see it. My aunt was the only one not in shock or scared.

Eventually, my mother did catch me and beat me in the middle of the bathroom. I was so loud that the other classes could hear me scream from down the hall that they came out asking what all the noise was. Ms. McDougal told them what was happening.

So, she beat me and yelled at me and told me to go back to class and that my aunt was going to take me home. Obviously, I didn't want to go back to class. I was too embarrassed, but she made me go.

The reason for the beating was that she had to leave work, which she didn't like leaving work cuz she lost out on money, because I got suspended off the school bus. So, now I had no way to get to school or get home. I was suspended for a week for singing graduation songs with my friends so I could get ready for an assembly. It was Lift Every Voice and Sing.

The bus driver, Larry, was a son of a bitch with a Jerry curl at the top, a fade on the sides and square duck's tail in the back. He also wore a cross earring. He looked stupid.

He said the singing was distracting. Mind you, I was getting fucked up on the bus every day, but that wasn't distracting, apparently. Plus, he would have music playing on a little radio all the time. He did tell us to be quiet, but we didn't like him, so we sang louder.

My screams and cries in pain might have been soothing for

him. Fuck him, he was an asshole.

The whole school talked about it for the full week, but I take it as a win, cuz I didn't have to take the bus either. I didn't get beat when I went home. So one beating for fourteen. I took it happily. I still would have done it again. I don't regret what happened, all things considered.

The other two girls got suspended too, but whatever their punishments were, wasn't as public or as embarrassing as mine.

21

Chapter 21

Dear Daughter,

At this time I was getting beat everyday on the bus and peeing in my bed every night because of the ghost dogs. I would just pray and I would hear this voice in my head saying that I was beautiful, and that I was special. I didn't understand it though.

I felt beautiful on the inside, but on the outside I was ugly. I know now that I was looking though mans eyes and not through the eyes of God.

It's hard to love yourself when everyone around you tells you that you are ugly. I would just pray that things would get better when I'm older or that God would take me in my sleep. I would wake up being disappointed to see another day.

Okay, when I was between eight and nine years old, my mother had a friend who was part of the project's softball team. My mother's friend had a daughter who was a couple of years older than me. We used to go over to her friend's house sometimes and have play dates. Her daughter's room looked like a Barbie Dream house, pink and white, really girly and beautiful. I want to have a room just like that. I never saw anything like it. This is where my love of the color pink came from, but it's also the room I got molested in so my feelings on it are kinda mixed. But we'll get to that in a minute.

She had an enormous bedroom with an adjoining playroom, with toys everywhere. She had a chest where there were clothes that we would play dress up with. She had so many dolls it was great, Like playing in a toy store.

She was so spoiled, but I loved being there.

One day she said, "We are going to play house. I'm going to be the daddy and you're going be the mommy".

I didn't like the way she looked at me. I can't really explain it, but I knew it wasn't going to be good.

"I'd rather play outside".

"No, it's fine. What you don't want to play with me? If you play, I'll let you take one of my dolls home o play dress up. You can pick anyone you like".

I still didn't really want to play, but I really wanted the doll. I only had ten, and they were Barbie.

So, we start to play the game and I'm pretending to cook with the toy stove, and I'm thinking this isn't so bad. She pretends to come home from work and gives me a kiss on the cheek. Then they say it's time to go to bed and I only know from TV that the parents go to sleep. Then she said we had to go into the closet. That seemed weird, but I went with her, anyway. My parents weren't together and my grandparents slept in two different rooms, so I just followed her lead cuz I didn't really know what regular parents did.

When we went into the closet, I pretended to get her a kiss goodnight so we could go to bed.

"No, not like that," she said, then she kissed me on the mouth.

I was thinking that's the stuff they only do on TV and it blew my mind.

"I don't like this. I don't wanna play this game anymore".

"Don't worry, I'll show you". That's when she started touching me.

I don't know where the adults were when all this was happening. I wanted to escape. I just didn't know how. I think they were in the living room playing cards and talking.

I was very confused, cuz I know I didn't like girls. It felt wrong, and I was too young to understand what was really happening. I didn't understand what she was trying to do cuz she was a girl. I only saw these things in movies and it was always a man and a woman. The movies I watched did give me a feeling that I couldn't figure out cuz again I was too young, but this feeling was different. Almost like dread.

We stayed in the closet for what felt like forever. It might have only really been an hour or so. After that experience, I didn't say anything about it. I didn't want to think about it and, based on the past, telling someone didn't feel safe.

One night, my mom asked me if I wanted to go back there for a sleepover. At first I didn't want to say anything. I just didn't want to go. This made her suspicious. I ended up telling her what happen, and she told her friend. I don't know what happened to her or how her parents reacted to what they heard. I know I didn't spend the night again until I was twelve years old.

I found out later that my god sister was molester by her uncle and a family friend. Her parents both knew, but they didn't think she would do anything to anyone else. They assumed that she just got over it and was embarrassed when they found out that she touched me in that way. She needed help, but her parents just thought that it would go away. I don't blame her or anything for what she did. I know that she didn't understand what she was doing or how it would affect me. She was only a few years older than me and shouldn't have had to go through that herself. It is a common chain that happens and needs to be dealt with properly so that it does not continue, but when things as serious as this get brushed off, they continue and more and more people get hurt.

When I went over there again, it was to give my mother a break, I guess, but I mainly lived with my grandmother, so whatever. I only stayed there for one night and it was okay at first. We played and everything was fine, but when it started getting late, she wanted to play house again and I wasn't playing this time. I asked my godmother if I could go to the bathroom, but I went to call my mother. I asked if she could come get me at 5 pm. I remember this clearly cause I was watching the clock, waiting for her.

I did spend other nights at her house after that, but I think she got the hint that I didn't want to play anymore and that I was older and said no and mean it. She didn't want to play with me much anymore cuz than she was playing with the boys on the block, so she left me alone. I wasn't going around with her when she did this. I just wanted to play hopscotch and double dutch.

I didn't want to play with the boys the way she was playing with them. The way she used to play with me. She thought I wasn't fun anymore and basically tried to peer pressure me into letting those boys touch me like they were touching her, but I didn't let them. I didn't care if she thought I was fun or whatever. I said no, and I meant no.

I didn't tell my mother what she was doing with those boys. It had nothing to do with me and her parents already told her not to do it, so what was my mother going to do that was going to change her mind? Nothing. She was doing what she wanted to do, and I played there as I wanted to and that was what parents expected their children to do at that age.

I didn't mind doing what my mother asked me to do and not to do. I was an obedient kid, considering all things. When I got older, I spread my wings, so to speak, but at this age I was not too proud to listen to the adults.

This caused us to kind of grow apart, but that's alright.

After my mother picked me up from her house for the last night, I found out that they moved several times. Don't know why they moved around so much. When I went over there, I always went with my mother and didn't spend the night no more. Cuz I was still going to west Virginia but before we went, I would spend two or three weeks with my Godmother, but after that summer I just went straight to West Virginia when school ended. I know it was boring in the south, but it was safer. Plus, I could watch whatever when I went down south, because they didn't monitor what I watched. They had cable and I could watch movies all night.

22

Chapter 22

Dear Daughter,

I guess I was just stupid, cause I thought I was just watching Rom-com, but I was watching things like Blue Lagoon, Scar Face, Porky, and Summer Lovers. I would watch these movies all night even though they were completely inappropriate, but I didn't know that.

It wasn't that they wanted me to watch these things, but there were distracted most of the time doing their own thing. I was old enough that they didn't see any harm leaving me in the room by myself while they entertained for friends or just played music and drinking in the living room. They just knew that I was quiet and kept to myself.

I don't know why no one in the 80s was monitoring what their kids were watching, like they didn't know what was on TV. I don't know if they just didn't think there was a problem with it or what.

Watching these things did give me feelings that i could figure out and without the proper guidance I had to figure it out for myself. I would watch these scenes and like it, but I knew I liked the men in the in the scenes, but at the same time I liked the women.

I felt happy for them. I didn't want to do that to another girl. I wanted to be her.

I wanted to be touched and held the way the guys were holding them. I was kind of jealous, but at this point I didn't expect to ever be looked at as if I was beautiful or any kind of desirable in the way I wanted to be desired, by someone I wanted to be desired by.

I lived through these movies. I wanted to be loved in a way that I never knew. In a way, I couldn't imagine was possible for someone like me.

I couldn't talk to anyone about all these emotions I was having. I didn't have anyone around me who I felt would understand. I grew up in a very religious family and if I tried to explain how I enjoyed seeing women in that state of bliss, they would have thrown the Bible at me. Instead of helping me or even understanding that I wasn't attracted to them in a conventional sense, they still would have thought I was homosexual.

I just kept my emotions to myself cuz I didn't want to deal with that. It's hard to explain complex feelings to simple people. Not everything is black and white. I have no sexual feelings for girls even though I was very confused because I was molested one, but I always knew I liked men. If nothing else, that experience helped me realize that I was not homosexual.

One weekend during the school year, when I was about ten years old, me and my friends would play tags. This was back in the city. Sometimes my mother would have me come back a few weeks before school started if I begged, so I could see my friends. Most of the time she only let me come back a weekend before school started cuz she said she needed the break.

I don't know what she was talking about cuz I was with my grandmother, anyway.

Some kids in the neighborhood were playing tag, but for some reason, one of the dirty kids changed the game to catch and hump. I didn't like playing games like that.

I just want to play tag. I didn't know that they changed the game cuz I was already running away.

We played boys vs girls like we did sometimes and one boy caught me behind the building and he grabbed me.

I was like, "okay, I'm it".

I expected him to run like anyone playing tag would do, but he grabbed me and started humping on me. I think he was younger than me, but he was taller and stronger than I was.

He humped me in the front, then spun me around and started humping me from the back.

"Let me go!". I didn't like it. He was dry humping me. I was crying and then when I screamed, he let me go.

I was shaking, and I ran in the house to tell my grandmother what happened, but one kid in the neighborhood told her that I was in the back of the building doing something dirty.

It was from one boy in the neighborhood, which was a complete lie. She didn't want to hear it. She beat me so badly and I was crying, trying to tell her what he did to me and that what she heard wasn't true. I tried to tell her that he grabbed me and that i didn't want to be touched like that. She thought I was lying.

I just wanted her to tell his mother and hug me and tell me it's going to be all right. But no, she beat me and then after she beat me.

I told my mother.

"Why you so Fast? You gonna grow up to have a house full of kids and end up on welfare, understand".

I went into my room and cried and prayed. I cried a lot when I was a kid. As I got older, I cried less and less, especially now I don't really cry at all.

I don't like to cry cuz it does nothing. People say crying is healthy and I agree, but sometimes crying just brings up hard memories that I don't want to deal with.

23

Chapter 23

Dear Daughter,

After that beating, I started to eat. I mean, I gained about fifty or sixty pounds during the school year. I would eat one of the industrial sized silver pots full of mac and cheese for dinner. I was ten years old and able to have two racks of ribs. By the time I was twelve years old, I was 125 pounds.

By the time I was about to go into the seventh grade, I had an eating disorder I would eat, then throw up. I decided that I wasn't going into the seventh grade fat. I used my aunt's work out bike and rode it every day. I thought that i was getting bullied cuz of my weight and I was done with that. I hated it.

I also had braces, and I got them out by that time, too. I was going to start junior high and I want to be a whole new person.

My grandmother was a big woman, so she just thought that I was a healthy eater.

One day I ask her, "Were you fat when you were a kid?".

"When I was your age, I was a cute size 16".

I was like, oh shit.

My mother didn't really care. She didn't think anything was wrong with me. She just told to stop eating so much. I asked her how I could lose weight and she was in her own world. She was trying to lose weight herself.

At that time, she was trying to lose her butt. It was natural and very big, but at that time it was the 80s and thin was in. She prioritized her boyfriends over worrying about what I was doing or trying to assist me.

I did lose a lot of weight by the time I started school that year. I did gain some of the back during the school year cuz I was eating snacks and such in the lunchroom.

I didn't want to gain the weight gain, so I started throwing up again.

That year around thanksgiving, my uncle followed me to the bathroom cuz I kept disappearing, and he found me throwing up. He told my grandmother, and she was so mad.

"Why you in there throwing all that god food?".

Mind you, they already knew that I wasn't happy with my weight and no was really helping me with it. My mother then took me to some type of workout program in the neighborhood so they could teach me how to eat healthy. It was the LA Weight Loss program. She didn't tell me where we were going and she just told me that a friend of hers told her about it.

It was someone from her job that told her about. I didn't know that he was talking about me like that at work, but whatever. She took me there instead of talking to me and put me in the program.

I'm happy that she did that for me instead of just ignoring that there was something wrong, but at the same time I would have liked it if she would have tried to talk to me about some of my issues. I guess she didn't know what to say, and this was the only thing she could think of to help.

My mother and my grandmother used to argue about the program. My grandmother thought my mother was stupid for paying for me to go to the program cuz she didn't think there was anything wrong with me. They also had me eating six meals a day that were portioned out and she thought that if I was trying to lose weight, why would they have me eating more often? She didn't understand the science behind it, even when my mother tried to explain it to her.

My mother stopped paying for the program for after a month cuz she listened to her mother, but I still kept the meal plans and still followed them.

At the same time I was dealing with the weight loss, around the beginning of the school year, a boy I was friends with asked me to be his girlfriends. It was the first time a boy took an interest in me in this way. His proposal shocked me and made me kinda happy, but I didn't want to be his girlfriend.

Everyone was trying to peer pressure me into being his girlfriend, but I didn't want to just walk around and pretend that I liked him when I knew I didn't. He was one of the cool kids too, but my friends were trying to use me to, in a sense, climb the social ladder of the school on my back.

I told him that I didn't see him that way. He asked me during homeroom, but by lunchtime, the entire school knew. After I told him no, all of his friends started to pick on me.

They weren't beating like I dealt with before, but that's when Felicia stopped talking to me cuz that was the cool kids she started hanging out with. Furthermore, his friend Dylan used to throw erasers at me when the teacher turned around, resulting in me being covered in chalk for the remainder of the day.

He used to spit in my food and put his finger in my milk carton.

In the seventh grade, near the fall, a boy moved into the projects with his aunt and cousin. I don't know why he moved there. I guess there was some family stuff going on, but whatever.

Anyway, he like me and asked me to be his girlfriend. I said yes happily, and we dated for about two weeks. In the beginning, when we first started dating, he asked if she could take me out on a date. I knew my mother would say no to the movies, but I asked him where he wanted us to go. He wanted to take me out to eat. I was twelve, about to turn thirteen, and he took me to White Castle.

I felt so grown up. I was so happy.

He asked my mother he could take me out to eat. Of course, she had to drive us.

"Are going to pay for it?".

"Yes, Ms. Linda".

She was cool with his aunt, so she was fine with us going on a date. He got money from his aunt and I was so excited.

She said sure and we head to the car. It was kinda late, and it was a delightful night. The other kids asked where we were going and I said he's taking me on a date. My mother was so proud, I think, and told everyone that she was coming to chaperon. Then she ruined the total effect by asking the other kids if they wanted to come.

About seven other kids jumped in the car. I was so pissed.

She said "It'll be fine".

They were talking about how they were going on the date with us and everyone was there. My cousin even came. It was my first date and the entire neighborhood was coming too. I didn't want their ass there.

When we get to White Castle, we try to find a table by ourselves.

My mother sits at the table with us, along with my cousin and another girl. We sat in the middle booth and we had kids in front of us and the back of us.

"Why did you bring all these people?".

"To make sure y'all don't do nothin".

"That's what you here for".

She ended up paying for all the other kids and when I asked if she was paying for us too she said, "No, he got you".

She was happy cuz all the kids would say she was so cool. I was mad cuz I don't know why she was trying to impress kids.

He tried to make me feel better, but I didn't want to hear it. Then she told the other kids when we got back to the block that I didn't have a good time and that I didn't want them there. Then they all came to asking if I really said that. I had to stand there and explain that I didn't mean that. I just wanted a nice time on a date not to have all my friends there.

They didn't talk to me for the rest of the week.

My mother just smirked at me with that fuck you over the way. "I guess they not really your friends then".

"Why would you tell them that".

"That's what you said, ain't it? It ain't got nothing to do with me".

That's when I realized that she just didn't like me. I knew she didn't love me, but I was like, really, you don't like me either. It was so fucked up.

24

Chapter 24

Dear Daughter,

One weekend, all the kids in the neighborhood decided to play man hunt. It was like twenty of us. Before that I asked my friend Tisha about kissing cuz I knew that Billy was going to try to kiss me. I just wanted to be prepared. She was a thin brown-skinned girl. She taught me how to tongue kiss using a compact mirror.

I thought I was ready to go there. Me and billy went into the building across from the one I lived in. We usually played in the buildings running up and down the stairs. It was nighttime and there were a lot of shot outs, so we were inside playing. Plus, all the adults were outside. It was an enormous building, so it was so exciting.

Me and Billy met up inside the staircase and then it happened. There were no butterflies or anything, but I was trying to follow him. I think I was concentrating so hard I couldn't really just enjoy it. I counted to twenty cause I didn't know how long it should last, but I felt like that was long enough.

It wasn't the most romantic first kiss, but I thought he was so cute and I was so happy he wanted to kiss me.

After the kiss, we tried to continue the game, but we didn't hear anyone. We left the building trying to find everyone, and they were all outside already sitting on the bench laughing and talking. Who caught who?

We were the last ones to come out of the building and everyone was wondering what we were doing in there. We can out holding hands and the girls ran up to me asking if he kissed me.

Our intention was to have a distraction away from the adults so we could have time alone to have our first kiss, so we planned the whole thing. My friend suggested that we play man hunt and me and Billy went off on our own. She knew how much I wanted to kiss him and know how our first date went so....

So all my friends we so excited that we kissed. So much was happening that I lost track of time. Me and my cousin were supposed to be home by 10 pm. She used to have this big train bell that used when she couldn't see us out the window and would ring it so that we knew to come home.

Billy was like, "What the hell is that?".

"That just means they have to go home," said one of my friends.

My cousin didn't even say anything. She just started walking back to our building. I was so embarrassed. Everyone knew about our bell. My grandmother was from the south and she used to use it for her kids, so she just felt like if it worked, why stop using it?

I couldn't wait till Monday to tell all my friends that I had my first kiss. Most people in my school were already fuckin, so I was considered behind sexually. Mind you, I was close to turning thirteen so...

My friends just told me congratulations.

From what my family told me, my cycle was supposed to come at the same time every month. They didn't teach me about the fact that it can be late for no reason or that it can change cycles. So I had it on my calendar and I knew I was supposed to get it on Tuesday, but I didn't get it.

So, I told my friend that I didn't get my period and she just told me to wait a couple of days. By this point, I would go with my friends for everything cuz they were a bit older, and they explained more than my family did.

By Friday, I went to school and told her that I still didn't get my period.

"Did you guys just kiss?".

"Yeah, we kissed, and he pulled me close. My grandmother told me when you kiss a boy, you get pregnant. Do you think I'm pregnant?" I asked her.

"I don't know, maybe. I heard that when you don't get your period, you're pregnant".

It was the blind leading the blind. I was so scared.

Saturday came, and I still didn't get my period. I didn't want to go outside and play cuz now I'm thinking I have to tell my grandmother that I'm pregnant.

Thinking of it now, the whole thing was so dumb. I know I didn't know, but it's still just so stupid.

I went in the kitchen and told my grandmother, "I'm pregnant".

She went from zero to one hundred freaking out. "Oh, lord, the girl done gone and ruined her life. Out there with them nasty little boys. I told Linda about you being out there past 9 o'clock. I ain't raising another baby".

Mind you, she didn't ask no questions. She was just ranting with herself. There was only me and her in the room, but she wasn't talking to me.

So, I'm just think I'm too young to have a baby. I was only in junior high and I just lost all that weight and babies make you fat.

I was like, how am I supposed to push a baby out of my butt? At this time, I didn't know anything about the female anatomy and I didn't know there were two holes.

I was like I have a hard time pooping, how am I gonna push a baby out of my ass?

My grandmother called my mother and told her that I was pregnant and so she came from work early. I remember cuz she walked in with her uniform on and she never came home with her uniform on.

"I guess you gonna be a grandma. I'm not raising another baby. You gotta deal with this".

My mother didn't say anything. She just laid on the couch in the fetal position and cried. She was crying cause she didn't know what she was going to do. Still, no one spoke to me. They just took my word for it. No one asked how I knew or anything.

While my mother was curled up on the couch, my grandmother called my aunt Bunny in West Virginia. She talking to Bunny and then suddenly she handed me the phone.

I really didn't want to speak to her cuz I was so ashamed. Bunny's and Buddy's opinion of me meant everything. I still didn't understand why my mother was crying, but I was afraid Bunny and Buddy would be mad at me. I was scared of my mother, but I respected Bunny.

So I got on the phone with Bunny, and she asked me questions.

"Where you with a boy?".

"Yes". I told her about the manhunt and how me and Billy were in the stairwell. At this time I started crying. I don't know the reason behind my tears, whether it was fear or something else.

"What did y'all do?".

"We kissed".

"What else?".

"With tongue", which made me cry even harder.

Shut up, it's not funny.

(Sorry).

"That's all. What else?".

"That's all, he put his tongue in my mouth". Mind you, I was ugly crying at this point. I thought that the stork was still real when I was in the fifth grade. I thought the stork brought the baby to the hospital and you pick it up with a number like at the market. I didn't know anything.

"Why do you think you're pregnant?".

"Well, Mama said that I get my period on the same day every month and I was supposed to get my period on Tuesday and it's Saturday. So I'm pregnant".

That's when her tone changed, and I knew she was mad. I thought she was mad at me.

"You're not pregnant. Stop crying. Put Mama on the phone".

I tried to stop crying and handed the phone back to my grandmother. I heard Bunny screaming into the phone at her. I caught bits and pieces of the conversation cuz she was so loud. I heard Buddy in the back ask what was happening and she just told him that she would tell him later.

The next thing I know, Bunny yelled, "That girl not pregnant!".

"How you know?".

I didn't hear anything after that, but I know Bunny was explaining the confusion.

"Where Linda at?".

"On the couch crying".

"Tell her to get her stupid ass off the couch and talk to the girl!".

My Grandmother and Bunny finished talking and told me to go to my room. I washed my face and laid down on the bed and later that night my period came.

The next day, when my mother was off, she acted like everything was normal, which was weird. She told me that on Monday I didn't have to go to school. I was happy cause I didn't want to go to school anyway, but I was confused. She told me that I was going to the doctor. I knew I already had my physical, so I didn't know why I had to go back.

The next day, I had my first gynecology appointment.

"Why am I here? What kind of doctor is this?".

"It's a doctor for women," my mother said.

So I went there, and I waited in the waiting room. When my name was called, I went in the room with the doctor. I wanted to my mother come in the room with me.

"Are you coming with me?".

"No, why I gotta go in there with you?".

"Cuz I don't know what's going on".

"That's he there for. Ask him what you wanna know".

"Okay".

I went into the room, still confused.

He started asking me questions. "What brings you here today?".

"I don't know".

Now the next part is gonna make you laugh, and I would have appreciated if you wouldn't.

(I will try, but I make no promises. Also, just for the record, this is not a funny book, but if you hear the delivery, it is hilarious and just kinda sad. I'm not a terrible person).

Oh, so you just wanna make that clear. Yeah, cuz the next part is kinda fucked up. Well, whatever. I like how you trying to explain yourself.

(I have to. Plus, she is laughing through most of this so. It's not just me laughing at her. I'm laughing with her about how sad the situation was and I also know or knew most of these people. Keep that in mind).

"I see that you're here today because you started your cycle".

"I don't know what you heard cuz my mother sold my bike years ago".

"What do you mean?".

"What do you mean?"

"I'm talking about your cycle".

"My bike was sold. I told you I don't ride".

He was confused as shit. I was confused. Why the was fuck a doctor talking to me about a bike for. I was like a comedy routine.

He said "Huh?".

I said "What?".

"Anyone ever told you about your period?".

"That's that ting that makes me bleed every month, right?".

"Give me one minute. I'm going to go out and talk to your mother really quick".

"Okay".

He came back in ten minutes later with the nurse. He examined my breast and my abdomen and asked me about the symptoms I had during my period.

I told him about the things that happened; you know, the throwing up and diarrhea and pain. After he did that, he should me a diagram of a woman's reproductive system and explained to me about how a woman gets there period every month.

I told him that sometime my period stayed for ten days and that sometimes it skipped a month. He told me that my period was irregular. He decided to put me on birth control pills.

"I'm not having sex".

"It's just to help regulate your period. Do you have any more questions?".

I was still wondering where babies come from, but I wanted to go home and I knew that later on that year we were going to start sex ed in school. I was excited about that.

I still didn't know about sperm and the egg or anything like that.

He gave me about of booklets about the reproductive system and periods and one about puberty. He talked to my mother, and we went home.

"Are you still confused?".

"A little".

"Well, it's too late. You should have asked him when you were in there".

My grandmother was mad when I got home cuz she thought cuz the doctor gave me birth control pills that he was giving me permission to do something.

"What you wanted me to do?".

"You her mother. You could've told him no".

I guess in their mind they thought I was gonna go out there and have sex. I thought I was pregnant from a kiss. Why would I do anything else? That when I knew that when it came to sex, the women in my family were no help. If I had a question about sex, I would ask my friends for everything. Other than that, I just learned from movies.

About a semester after that, I learned about how people get pregnant. I would always pay attention in sex ed class.

After sex ed, they told me to talk to your parents about it if you had questions.

So, I went home and tried to talk to my mother.

"Can We talk about sex?".

"Sure, what you wanna know?".

"Does it hurt?".

"Yes, don't do it. Good talk", then she got up and walked away.

I don't know why I listened to my teacher and tried to talk to my mother. It was stupid.

25

Chapter 25

Dear Daughter,

When I was in the eighth grade, I was on the swing and you know how you stand up so you can go higher than you jump off. I was trying to do that, but before I could slow down enough to jump off, someone yanked the seat of the swing from underneath my feet and I went flying.

I hit the pavement on my back near the fence and I was home in a back brace for two months. It looked like a straitjacket.

They couldn't do much because my back wasn't broken, it was just sprained badly.

He did get suspended for a week and after that; he did leave me alone. I think he kinda felt bad for what happened cuz the ambulance had to come to the school and everything.

I begged Bunny and Buddy if I could go to the school in West sprained, but they said no cuz the school system in the south was slower than in the city and I would be like two years ahead.

The kids just kinda ignored me after that.

There was a security guard there named Weasel, who used to

always stand up for me. In the sense, he would tell people to leave me alone. He said he looked out for me cuz he knew the family. I didn't know there was something behind that, but I'll get to that later.

In eighth grade after that incident, Ms. Kienan would take a few people out of lunch for about an hour and we would study math. If we didn't finish lunch, we could take it with us. It was me and a few other people, but more notably David.

People regarded him as very handsome and he had a history of dating black girls. We became close friends. We were friends with everyone there, but we became closer. He did date one of my friends before we became from, but she broke up with him for Dylan. I don't know why, but whatever.

He was broken-hearted, and I was his shoulder to cry on. I liked him, but I didn't think he liked me back. He thought that I was funny.

At the time I didn't fist fight, but I was very good at playing dozens. If you don't know what that is, it's just a game where you go back and for and insult each other. The one who has nothing to say or gets their feelings hurt first loss. I'm still great at that game, as you know.

I taught all of you how to play it, maybe too well.

He said the way I looked at the world was funny. My family just thought that I was rude.

He said that I made him feel better about the breakup and we started hang out after school.

I like making him laugh cuz he had the prettiest smile I ever seen.

He introduced me to a lot of music like AC/DC, Poison, Bon Jovi, etc. I tried to introduce him to Hip Hop, but knew more than I thought he would.

After school one day, he was listening to Poison, and we were just hanging out. It's so clique, but something flew in my eye and he tried to blow it out.

"Did I get it?".

"Yeah". We stood there a minute, looking into each other's eyes. It was so romantic. Then he just gave me a quick peck. I just looked at him and my mouth dropped.

"Sorry. Are you OK?".

"Yeah, I think so".

It was real fast and he kind of head butt me more than kissed me. His teeth hit my teeth. After the initial shock, I was just hoping that someone saw it. Just so people knew that he liked me, not so it was like my first date of anything.

I felt like it was my birthday. Well, not like my birthday I guess cuz I didn't celebrate my birthday, but how it was supposed to feel. I don't have much to compare the feeling to, but you get the point.

"Can I do it again?".

"Yes".

When he kissed me this time, I didn't count. I think it was love, but I felt like I had to throw up. I was happy, but I think my nose started running and I felt sick. My hands got clammy. I didn't know what was happening to me, but I didn't want to do or be anywhere else.

After the kiss, he asked me to go to the movies on our first date. I don't remember what movie it was, but I know Micheal J. Fox starred in it. I lied and told my mother that i was going to movies with a couple of my friends, but I took the bus and met him in front of the theater.

It was nice, but we were both nervous. I almost lost my mind cause we shared a big container of popcorn and a drink. I didn't want to go home cause it was still early.

"Have you ever bowled before?".

"No", I said nervously.

I wasn't nervous about bowling, I just thought it was unsanitary to wear strange shoes. That day, he taught me how to bowl. I still love top go bowling and I'm pretty good at it.

Wii bowling is my shit.

When we finished bowling, he wanted to take me home, but I politely declined and he walked me to the bus stop.

"You don't want me to go to your neighborhood".

"No, it's OK".

"Are you ashamed?".

"Yup".

"Why? I'm not scared of the projects".

"Have you ever been to the projects?".

"No".

"Then no".

He said, "I'll let you come to my house some day".

"OK".

One day, I did let him walk me to Jamaica Avenue. That was the place where everyone goes to shop and hang out.

He did not embarrass me. I just knew how other people would react to seeing me with a white boy. I didn't want to hear it, and I was ashamed of where I lived. He came from a wealthy family and lived in a pleasant house. I didn't want him to see where I lived and did not want to be with me anymore.

My grandmother knew that I was dating a white guy and so did my aunt Bunny and uncle Buddy. I didn't tell my mother cuz I didn't think she cared.

My grandmother usually had an issue with me dating, but didn't have a problem with him cuz he was white. As long as he was white and had money, it was OK.

It's not like he had a job or anything. We were too young, but whatever. I didn't care that he had money or came from a well off family. He was sweet and caring and handsome. He was also one of the smartest people I knew.

We dated for about three months. It was around mother's day and he asked if I wanted to meet his mom. By this time I already met his dad, but it was quick cuz I only went in his house to use the bathroom. He had an apartment that was on a very high floor, and they had a den and a library. I only thought they had those in movies. I never saw something like that before.

"Sure".

"OK, I think it'll be great since you already met my dad".

His dad was a nice man, about 5'6, with reddish blond hair and a cute smile. I can see where David got it from. He was very nice to me. He seemed a bit shocked to see that I was black, but he didn't seem to care. Maybe he didn't take that seriously cuz we were just kids, but David's happiness came first for him.

The day before the mother's day dinner, he thought it was a good idea for me to meet his mom. The dinner was at Toni Romas on Queens boulevard, a fancy rib place.

That day I tried to dress presentable for her. I wore a corduroy skirt that was just below my knees, a white button-up shirt, stockings and black shoes.

He had a white shirt, khaki pants, and brown penny loafers. It was funny cause he actually put a penny in it. We used to argue about that. Now it seems so dumb, but we were really mad at each other.

"why do you put a penny in your shoes".

"Cause they're penny loafers".

"So, they don't come with a penny inside".

"How can they be penny loafers without the penny".

"That's stupid".

We went to his building. He introduced me to his doorman.

"Hello, Ms. McClain. How are you?". No one has ever addressed me by my last name before.

"Are my parents upstairs?".

"Would you like me to tell your parents that you have a guest?".

"yes. It would be good to give them a heads up".

It confused me cuz why did you have to announce that you have someone coming over to your house?

We got in the elevator, and he lived on the 18th floor.

"Are you OK?" he asked.

"Yes". I was lying, my thighs were sweating.

He kept trying to hold my hand, but I kept taking it back to try to get the sweat off of them cuz they were so clammy.

When we reached the door, he rang the doorbell cuz he would always lose his keys. His father answered the door with a smile and let up in.

"Hello, Deneque. How are you?".

"Fine sir. How are you?" I responded nervously.

"So, I heard David wants to invite you to the mother's day dinner. Usually it's just family, so he must really like you. Are you happy to come?".

"Yes. I guess, he just told me that I should meet his mother before I show up".

"Yes, that would be best".

It all felt so secretive, but I didn't think too much about it. I thought that was just how white people did things.

My and his dad had some small talk and David kept whispering in my ear asking me if I was OK. I was starting to get annoyed, but didn't want to yell at him in front of his father. It was starting me make me worry, even though I felt like I was doing fine.

After talking for a bit, his father told me to take a sit. I thought they're living room was nicer than my grandmother's cuz it didn't have plastic. It was nice cuz I didn't have to worry about my legs sticking since I was in a skirt.

I took a sit and David sat next to me.

"Would either of you like a drink? We have water, iced tea, and we have wine and spirits, but I think you're too young for that," he said merrily.

I laughed even though it was all that funny, but he was sweet.

I took the ice tea, and he whispered to me "Good choice".

"Why?".

"Cause he likes to brag about his iced tea".

While his father was preparing to serve the tea, he went on and explained that he made his tea from scratch, not like instant tea like other people do. He used tea leaves. I didn't know about infusing tea leaves to make tea other than in Chinese movies. I didn't know people actually did that.

"David, go in the back and ask your mother if she's read to meet Deneque".

"I'll be right back", and he kissed me on the cheek before getting up and heading toward the back.

It was sweet, but I hoped his father didn't see it.

"She's coming now".

His father was about to ask me how school was, but mid-sentence, I heard his mother coming down the hall. She had blond hair, about the same height as his father, with blond hair, and green eyes. I was like looking at Barbie and Ken.

Her eyes lit up cuz I guess she didn't expect me to be black, even though my name should have given me away.

I stood up when she entered the room, but David and his father stood up when they heard her shoes.

She smiled at me and sat next to her husband across from me and David. they had two couches that were separated by a coffee table that stood on top of an oriental rug.

"So, David wants you to come to our mother's day dinner, but aren't you doing something with your mother".

David was about to answer for me, but when he opened his mouth she said, "I'm asking Deneque".

"Yeah, but we do the same thing every year. We go to church, then we go to the Chinese buffet".

"I understand, but mother's day is supposed to be for family".

"I thought it would be nice if she came this one time, since she doesn't like being with her family," David said.

"Wouldn't your mother be upset?".

"Well, I already told her that I might go with David's family for mother's day and she said that it's fine".

"Why wouldn't she mind you spending mother's day with a different family?".

"I don't know, she just doesn't care," I responded.

"Where exactly do you live again? David told me that live in south Jamaica, but he didn't tell me exactly where," she asked suspiciously.

Now David started to squeeze my hand to where I had to snatch my hand away.

"I live in south Jamaica houses".

"What is that?".

Her husband said, "You know the apartment complexes".

"Oh".

She kept asking me random questions about my family; it was like a job interview. I thought it went well.

His father asked, "What are you guys gonna do today?".

"We are going to 7/11 then going bowling," David replied.

To me, it seemed like the perfect date. We were only at his house for about an hour, even though it felt longer.

"Are you ready to go?".

"Yes. It was nice to meet you," I told his parents.

They both told me it was nice to meet me as well, but I knew his mother didn't mean it.

His father gave him a fifty, and I tried to make a joke about it and everyone laughed except his mother, who rolled her eyes.

As we went to the elevator he said, "I think it went well".

"You sure? What about your mother?".

"That's just how she is".

The whole elevator ride, he was talking about something, but I wasn't paying attention. My mind was running, thinking if she liked me or not.

When we got to the lobby, the doorman told David that his mother wanted him to go back upstairs for something.

"For what?".

"I'm not sure, sir. She just requested that you go back upstairs".

"Deneque, come on".

"No. Your mother wants to only talk to you. She said that she can wait here. Don't worry, I'll watch her. She'll be fine".

With that, I sat down on the brown couch in the lobby.

He didn't say anything, he just smiled and went back into the elevator.

I waited for David to come back, and the doorman kept looking at me. It was like he knew something, but couldn't tell me. He was a short black man. When we did make eye contact, we just smiled at each other awkwardly. To this day, I still want to know

119

what he was thinking. If he knew what was going to happen or if he wanted to warn me.

He was upstairs for about a half an hour and when he returned; he looked kinda pissed.

"Everything alright?".

"I'll tell you later".

"OK".

"I don't wanna go bowling anymore".

"OK, what do you wanna do?".

"Let's go to the movies".

"To see what?".

"I don't care".

I thought it was weird, but I was willing to do whatever he wanted to do.

So, we went to the movies, and I continued to ask him if everything was OK, but he walked in silence. We got to the movies and the only thing that was playing was Bill and Ted Excellent Adventure. We were waiting to see that movie anyway, so we went to see that.

During the movie, he smiled a little, but every time I tried to hold his hand, he snatched his hand back.

"Are you mad at me?" I asked.

"No".

"Why don't you want to hold my hand?".

"Fine, you want me to hold you hand".

Then he grabbed my hand and squeezed it. It hurt and i was still so confused.

I snatched my hand away, and he took back, but this time he held it gently and apologized.

Now I'm not paying attention to the movie at all. I'm wondering what happened between him and his parents.

After the movies, he walks me to the bus stop and gives me a peck. This time he kissed me longer than usual, which was weird cause he didn't like kissing in public. Then he gave me a hug which he's never done before and I got on the bus.

When that Monday came, he wasn't there. I asked his friends if they saw him and they said he didn't say anything about not coming to school when they talked to him over the weekend.

Between classes, I called his house just to see if he was alright, but no one answered. Both of his parents worked, but I figured that he would be home. I went home worried and tried not to stress too much and thought I would just see him in school tomorrow.

We had a couple of classes together, but he didn't really speak to me. I asked if he was OK and he said that he would speak to me during lunch. By lunch time there was a rumor going around that me and David broke up.

Now I'm pissed and I couldn't wait till lunch. How am I the last person to know that my relationship has ended? I was too upset to be embarrassed.

When I finally saw him at lunch, I asked him, "What happened?".

He pulled to the side in the lunchroom and said, "I can't see you anymore".

"Why? What did I do?".

"Nothing".

"I just want to go to college and I have plans".

"OK, but we're in Junior high. What are you talking about?".

Now he's stumbling over his words and trying to explain to me his future plans. I know all this already and I didn't understand what it had to do with us. Basically, his mother threatened to cut him off if he didn't stop seeing me. He had a college fund and a trust fund and he wouldn't get any of it if we stayed together.

His father didn't have a problem with us because he was like we were just kids, but his mother saw that he was serious about me and wanted to stop it before it went any further.

I this mother didn't care too much about the fact that I was black, but more about where my family lived and that we were poor. She might have been a bit racist as well, but how David explained it was that it was cuz of my family. David tried to explain to her that I was not like my family and that I was smart, but she didn't want to hear that.

"We could just be together without everyone knowing".

"You found out that I was going to break up with you before I told you. How are we supposed to sneak around without someone finding out?".

I knew that his friends knew his parents, and that wasn't a risk he was willing to take.

"We can still be friends".

"I hate you. Fuck you".

Looking back at it now, he was so hurt. Back then, I just thought he was a coward.

When we went into the lunchroom, he went back to his table and I went back to mine. I saw all his friends whispering and looking at me. I ended up faking a stomach ache and asked to go home.

When I got home, my grandmother asked me what was wrong, and I told her that I just didn't feel well. That night I called my aunt Bunny and told her everything that happened.

She tried to comfort me as best as she could, but eventually she put Buddy on the phone, thinking that it might be better hearing it from a man.

By the time Buddy got on the phone, I was crying like someone had died. He tried to explain to me about money and status and that it might not have been all about race. He tried to tell me that David was hurting too, even though I didn't want to hear that. I was thinking that I never wanted to speak to him again.

Eventually, we did get to a place where we were fine, but it took a while. We would sneak glances at each other. I hated him and his whole family. I wished we never went to his family cuz maybe we would have still been together. In my mind, I wanted to run away together. I also felt some resentment towards my family for being poor.

I just became angry. After I got over the anger towards his family, I started blaming my own. I would slam doors and blame them for ruining my life.

There was a couple of weeks before school was over when one of my friends asked me "Are you still a virgin?".

"Yes. Why?" that's when they started laughing.

"Well, we're going to be senior next year. You can't be a virgin and a senior. Don't you ever want a boyfriend again".

"Of course".

"Then promise me you'll loss your virginity this summer".

"What if I can't find anyone?".

"Then you would ever get a boyfriend".

They explained to me that I needed to come back as a woman for my senior year. Of course, I wanted it to be with David, but that was over so. I didn't want to do anything with the boys in the neighborhood. That's when I thought of West Virginia. I agreed to their challenge and they would want details, so I couldn't make it up. My original plan was to watch a movie and tell them what I saw, but now that didn't seem like an option.

My new goal was to not come back to New York without losing my virginity. Operation to come back as a woman began.

To be Continued...

About the Author

Deneque White currently lives in New York, NY. She's a divorced mother of four and a grandmother of three. Founder, COO, and co-owner of Eli-Rose LLC.

Linda Grinvalsky currently lives in Fall River, Massachusetts. She is a wife and mother of one. CEO and co-owner of Eli-Rose LLC.